REACH FOR MORE

A Journey from Loss to
Love AND Fulfillment

By
David M. Szumowski

Author
David M. Szumowski

Style Editor and Graphic Design
Kristin Bryans, ArtSmart Communications

Cover Inset Photo
"Bridge Beams" by Phil R. Fitzgerald
Fitzgerald Visuals | www.fitz-visuals.com

Publisher
Wayne Dementi
Dementi Milestone Publishing, Inc.
Manakin-Sabot, VA 23103
www.dementimilestonepublishing.com

ISBN
978-1-7325179-5-0

Library of Congress Control Number: 2019930026

Printed in the USA

Dedication

To my wife Janice

Your entry into my life rescued me from despair and depression. Your love and support for the last 42 years has sustained me and given my life meaning beyond words. With deepest love and gratitude, thank you for loving me.

Acknowledgments

This book could not have been completed successfully without the input, advice, modification suggestions, proofing, and encouragement of the following individuals. You know your role in assisting with this project. I thank you all very much.

Janice Szumowski
Kristin Bryans
Jennifer McKee
Judy Basinski
Wayne Dementi
BG John C. Bahnsen (US Army Retired)
Colonel Marilyn J. Sylvester (US Army Retired)
Reverend Edward Harrison (Episcopal Priest Retired)
Tony Maino
Edward Checkert
Urban Miyares
Patrick Russell
K. Richard Sinclair

Affirmations

David's appointment to the court as a blind judge surprised most of the San Diego bench. He proved quickly that his criminal law experience, work ethic, attention to detail, and acceptance of his share of the work was not impaired by his disability. Szumowski's legal career has been as inspiring to our community as has been his life's story after losing his eyesight in Vietnam. His 18 years of service to this bench was an inspiration to all of us.

- Tony Maino
San Diego Superior Court Judge

What was the boss thinking when he hired this blind guy? How is he going to stand in front of a jury and present physical evidence like photos, diagrams and weapons when he can't see them himself? How will he be able to judge the demeanor of witnesses? These were among the questions I asked myself when David and I were assigned to the same office. The answers came quickly. Through dedication, hard work, long hours, and an intuitive grasp of basic human nature, he proved to me that he could do it and do it very well.

- Ed Checkert
Deputy District Attorney (Retired)
San Diego, CA

Read your book and found it fascinating...only wishing I had this book available when I first went blind. It surely would have helped me through the early depression years of blindness.

When comparing our lives, your story is quite different than my story, especially our growing up years. The boy from the country and the boy from the city...although there are a number of similarities — such as Mickey Mantle.

Your book should be required reading by anyone who loses their sight, especially those in blind rehabilitation.

Good job; loved the book.

- Urban Miyares
Blinded Veteran, Businessman

Adapt and overcome. The combat mantra. A great guide for war and not a bad one for a civilian life.

Dave is the ultimate practitioner. From a promising career in the Army (or elsewhere) to a world where you start over in rehabilitation. A world that takes your vision and moves you off the success track. Not for Dave. It was simply another challenge with some different twists. From veteran leader to successful prosecution attorney to Superior Court Judge, Dave adapted and overcame by courage, resiliency and warrior spirit.

Along the way, Dave developed a sense better than vision. Insight. It was not a gift, it was the result of hard work and dedication. It was what made him a great judge and role model. It is a remarkable life.

- Patrick C. Russell
Retired Military and
Retired Law Enforcement Officer

Dave was my college roommate and we pledged our fraternity together. I have now known him for 55 years.

We spent our last week together in San Francisco, living life to its fullest, before we each left for a year in Vietnam. His year was much shorter than mine. While he might have been a career Army Officer, life took a different turn for him. He could have thrown in the towel at age 23, but he didn't and his life has been one of inspiration for me and for all those who have known him. Getting through law school would be hard enough, but becoming a successful judge is another dimension.

Every year, we meet to play golf in Florida. People are almost overwhelmed by his enthusiasm for the game of golf and for the game of life. I communicate with him almost every day, in one form or another and I love his wit and his wisdom and his intellect which has been honed from all of his experiences.

Life is full of challenges for all of us — Dave just refuses to see any of them as roadblocks.

- Richard Sinclair
Lifelong College Friend, Veteran

Judge Szumowski is an icon of courage, determination, and sheer grit in the face of a life-changing adversity. This is one heck of an inspirational story told by a real American hero. Dave Szumowski is an inspiration to anyone who meets him...as a man, as a soldier, and as a judge. Here is a fair-haired, good-looking, fun-loving young man who was suddenly blinded in Vietnam. Here is an incredible story of how he had to dig deep into himself to find out who he really was, what he was really made of, and what kind of life he wanted to have. Truly inspirational!

- The Rev. Edward Harrison
Judge Szumowski's former priest

John C. "Doc" Bahnsen was born on November 8, 1934, in Albany, Georgia. He entered the U.S. Military Academy at West Point, New York, on July 1, 1952, and was commissioned a 2d Lt of Infantry on June 5, 1956.

He was Commander of the Air Cavalry Troop and then 1st Squadron with the 11th Armored Cavalry Regiment in South Vietnam from September 1968 to September 1969, the period during which David Szumowski served.

Brigadier General Bahnsen was one of the most highly decorated officers of the Vietnam War. His awards include Distinguished Service Cross, Silver Star (5), Distinguished Flying Cross (3), Legion of Merit (4), Bronze Star (4), Air Medal (51), Purple Heart (2) and the Meritorious Service Medal.

He is author of American Warrior: A Combat Memoir of Vietnam, with Wess Roberts, foreword by H. Norman Schwarzkopf.

Foreword

by John C. "Doc" Bahnsen

20 March 1969 Michelin Rubber Plantation, near Dau Tieng, Republic of South Vietnam. I commanded the Air Cavalry Troop of the 11th Armored Cavalry Regiment, "Blackhorse". It was a day of heavy combat with North Vietnamese forces located in bunkers in a jungle just outside the rubber trees of the Michelin plantation. The regiment had ordered a B-52 strike on the suspected enemy complex and it was my duty to perform a Bomb Damage Assessment (BDA) of the strike. The Regimental Air Cavalry Troop consisted of about 300 soldiers, 26 helicopters and an Aero-rifle platoon of 42 elite infantrymen. Ten OH-6 Scout helicopters, Nine AH-1 Gunships and Seven UH-1 lift ships were our authorized helicopters. I routinely commanded from a UH-1 helicopter, but on many occasions landed and commanded units on the ground.

The BDA mission started with scout helicopters overflying the strike area backed up by gunships circling overhead. Upon a quick assessment of the area, camouflaged bunkers were noted and I ordered my Aero-rifle platoon to be placed on the ground to further assess the damage and if possible, to make contact with the enemy. The platoon landed and moved towards the area and was taken under fire. One of our new squad leaders, SGT Frank D.P. Saracino, Jr. was killed with the initial burst of fire and several others were wounded. Saracino was walking point and the others could not get to him to recover his body. The platoon leader, newly assigned and on his first contact mission, hunkered down and called for reinforcement. I immediately contacted the Air Force FAC (Forward Air Controller) requesting air strikes on the enemy area. I ordered the platoon leader to hold his position while I brought in fighters to bomb the area, and contacted Regiment and asked for armored forces to be moved to my location. The nearest units were elements of the 3rd Squadron, 11th Armored Cavalry Regiment. This build up of forces was Standard Operation Procedure (SOP) for the regiment under command of Colonel George S. Patton.

Regiment chopped (ordered) a tank platoon of 5 tanks, an ACAV (Armored Cavalry Assault Vehicle) platoon and an infantry company to me from the 3rd Squadron, commanded by LTC John McEnery. The forces were located several kilometers from my location and had to proceed through heavy jungle to get to me. The tank platoon of 5 M-48 tanks was lead by LT David Szumowski.

It took a couple of hours to get this force into the contact area. I guided the force from my helicopter and got them in touch with the Aero-rifle platoon leader. I hastily gave orders for the force to attack into the bunker complex with the tank platoon in the lead — five on line, followed closely by the infantry company which had been air landed into the area. At that point things fell apart. The tank platoon started through the bunker area firing as they went, but the infantry company did not follow close behind them. As the tanks moved forward without close infantry support covering their rear, the enemy exited their bunkers and attacked the tanks with Rocket Propelled Grenades (RPG-7s). Four of the five tanks were hit and a couple rolled into bomb craters. 3 of them were on fire and the other one disabled. LT Szumowski was blinded and was on the radio telling me what happened. He was in a great deal of pain and needed to be evacuated, as did a number of his men. The sole remaining tank came up on my radio net and I gave him directions to circle back to the starting point.

At that point I contacted LTC McEnery and gave him a situation report and told him I was critical on fuel and had to leave the area. He immediately assumed command, landed his Scout helicopter in the area and brilliantly and bravely organized the forces and mounted the single operational tank and led the tank-infantry force into the bunker complex. The end result was 131 dead enemy soldiers. SGT Saracino was killed in action and a large number of soldiers were wounded.

I returned to the area and witnessed this action. LTC McEnery was wounded and he along with the others were evacuated to the 93rd Evacuation Hospital in Long Binh. I did not know David Szumowski at the time, but knew he was hit the eyes during the action. I learned of his total blindness many years later. This book tells the story of that young Lieutenant's loss of his eyes and the extraordinary life he has led since that tragic wounding.

I will not go into the Vietnam War and all the feeling about it by our generation. Suffice to say that over 55,000 Americans died in the War and millions of Vietnamese paid with their lives. Thousands of Americans suffered serious wounds and many still carry the scars both physically and mentally. Until the day I die I will carry the burden of 44 soldiers being killed under my command. Every one was a tragedy in my eyes — average age 19. David Szumowski is one of the true heroes of our generation in that as a young man he suffered what could have been a total show stopper for a full and complete life. His story is one of perseverance and love and loyalty and grit and determination and success in his chosen field.

He does not know the word quit, nor the phrase give up and he does not use excuses when things do not go his way. My admiration knows no bounds in reading his story. Little did I know about a young American lieutenant tank platoon leader who did his duty leading his soldiers in combat not knowing the way that action would impact the rest of his life. Our country is blessed to have men and women willing to fight our nation's battles and to risk their future to ensure the freedoms and privileges we enjoy.

John C. "Doc" Bahnsen

John C. "Doc" Bahnsen
Brigadier General, US Army (Retired)

Marilyn J. Sylvester was born on October 10, 1938 in Seattle, Washington. She graduated Magna Cum Laude from Seattle University earning her a baccalaureate degree in nursing in 1961. In 1965 she earned her master's degree in nursing at the University of Washington.

In November of 1965 she was commissioned as an ILT in the Army Nurse Corps. Her first overseas assignment was at US Army Hospital, Camp Zama, Japan.

Her next assignment was as Assistant Professor of Nursing at Walter Reed Army Institute of Nursing (WRAIN) — University of Maryland.

June 1977, she attended Command and General Staff College at Fort Leavenworth, KS. Only one or two nurses per year attend this collage.

Later she was Chief, Department of Nursing at the 196th Station Hospital, Belgium. Medical care was provided to military personnel and their families from the 15 countries which comprised SHAPE (Supreme Headquarters Allied Powers Europe).

April 1988 Colonel Marilyn J Sylvester retired from the Army following

Preface

by Marilyn Sylvester

I am the Army Nurse who cared for David Szumowski at US Army Hospital, Camp Zama, Japan. Despite being blinded while in combat, he demonstrated exceptional courage. He was calm, cooperative, and had a good sense of humor. He appreciated all that we did for him.

Once he was transferred to Walter Reed Army Hospital in Washington, DC we exchanged letters for several years; I was anxious to find out how he was doing.

I recall that he attended a rehabilitation center for the blind at Edward Hines, Jr. VA Hospital in Chicago. Not long after that he entered law school in Denver, CO. Shortly after he graduated from law school, we lost track of each other. There were times when I thought of him and wondered how and where he was.

Once retired, David decided to write a book about his life. While writing the book *Reach for More*, he decided to try and find me. He had several people helping him in this endeavor.

He remembered that I was from Washington State. With the help of the internet, he discovered that I had started a scholarship: Colonel Marilyn J. Sylvester, Retired, Endowed Scholarship at the Seattle University College of Nursing. He spoke with a person employed at the College of Nursing requesting that she call me and give me his phone number.

I immediately called David and was astonished to hear his voice. It was an exceptionally long phone call as we had so much to say. He sent me a rough draft of the book *Reach for More*.

I was overwhelmed to learn of his many accomplishments, and I believe you will also feel this way.

David was once my patient, but now I feel we are becoming friends.

Marilyn Sylvester

Introduction

David M. Szumowski

In 1969, my life changed drastically. I grew up as the first child of the post-war generation. My parents both were in the army and served in France during WWII. They knew the horror of war, and sought a safe and normal life for the family to come. My lower middle class upbringing was in upstate New York. It was a typical home life for the baby boom generation. Hard work by parents, hard play and education for children, religious teachings and moral values constituted the foundation for a successful life.

I was the first of my generation to attend college and there, gravitated to a military experience from ROTC. America was in Vietnam.

I went to Vietnam in 1969 and forty days later, life as I expected it to be changed forever. I returned home with one less important sense. I would learn to live life without sight.

This is my story of gradually accepting the change in my life. It is also the story of depression, anxiety, a testing of my faith, struggles accepting blindness, finding opportunity and overcoming obstacles on the road to a career in law culminating with my retirement as a judge.

For the next forty years, opportunities and challenges presented themselves to me and I met them successfully. This is my story of loss, resilience, and perseverance against the odds. It is also a story of support, love and devotion from my family, my wife, my lifelong friends, and six loyal and trusted Seeing Eye guide dogs. Without them, this memoir of a life fulfilled would not be worth recounting. I hope this book inspires the disabled, the religious, the military and veterans, and the general public to understand that success results from playing the hand you are dealt, seizing opportunities that present themselves, having faith in God and never giving up.

Prologue

Game Changer

March 19, 1969 — It was a typical spring day in South Vietnam. The heat was stifling, the air was filled with dust and the choking smell of diesel fuel fumes from the exhaust of our tanks. But we knew the monsoon season was coming, and soon we would be tank-tread deep in mud as we tried to stay dry.

I was standing in the turret of my 48-ton tank, with my head and shoulders exposed above its armor plate, wearing my flak jacket and tank helmet wired into the radio as we rolled through the sparsely inhabited terrain. The five tanks of the armor platoon I commanded were on a combat patrol with the mission of finding enemy troops infiltrating from the Ho Chi Minh Trail, across the Cambodian border, into III Corps, one of the four tactical zones in Vietnam. We were the second platoon of M Company, a tank company of the 3rd Battalion of the 11th Armored Cavalry Regiment.

While patrolling, my platoon was ordered to move to the westerly side of the Michelin rubber plantation in III Corps of South Vietnam. While getting there, we had seen dust and dirt and not much else as we patrolled roads looking for evidence of North Vietnamese activity in the area. Occasionally we would see a grouping of small mooches which housed local families. Most of the local people stopped their daily task to watch the huge tanks roll past, churning up dust as they passed. We could not tell if they were friendly to Americans by day and then became the enemy at night. We were always alert to an ambush. We never let down our guard.

We were a mixture of experienced combat soldiers and some newer replacement troops which included me. I had been in one brief fire fight, so my rookie status had been tested already.

We were ordered to take up a secure (defensible) position for the night. I was advised by a radio call that there were going to be serious fireworks through the night, and we had to be buttoned up tight with hatches closed.

That night, the B52 bombers carpet bombed the portion of the Ho Chi Minh Trail in our vicinity. It is a strange feeling to believe you are secure in a 48-ton vehicle when suddenly you are bombarded with tremendous noise. Our tanks were rocking back and forth from the concussion of exploding bombs a mile away. We would be on patrol tomorrow in the bombed area for damage assessment, cleanup, body count and confiscation of weapons and contraband.

The sound of those bombs going off is similar to what I might hear in a movie of the D-Day landings on the beaches in France at the Normandy invasion. I felt sorry for anyone within lethal bomb radius range of those 500 pound bombs.

In the morning, we began a patrol in the area covered by the bombing. Giant bomb craters dotted the landscape. Areas took on a moonscape appearance. There were large rocks, small rocks, and huge craters 25 feet across and 10 feet deep. Negotiating our tanks through the area was tricky, as no one wanted to have to pull out a 48-ton tank from a crater. Without knowing the enemy situation, that task presented a security danger.

As we patrolled, we saw discarded weapons, backpacks, rice cookers, dead enemy bodies and other remnants of enemy activity. With the heat and humidity, the stench of death was palpable.

Suddenly my radio squawked in my headset. "Green Inning 26, this is Green Inning 6, over" came the call from the company commander. "Green Inning 26, over" I responded using my designated call sign for the month. The Captain in command of our company replied, "This is 6. Headquarters has chopped you off your current mission and has a report of an infantry platoon pinned down a few miles from you. They have one man down and cannot get to his body due to heavy fire from a series of enemy bunkers firing at them from many sides. You are to proceed to their position and try to use the tanks as a blocking force between the Dinks and those pinned down so they can retrieve their man. Then, help them take out the enemy, over."

The Captain gave me the map coordinates, and my platoon started the several thousand meter ride to assist the ground soldiers.

It took our 5 tanks an hour or so to travel the few miles to the location of the fire fight because of having to maneuver through rough terrain and jungle. Once on scene, the platoon leader in charge of the ground unit came up on my tank and explained the situation. He said his man was just around the next turn, but the enemy fire was coming from a bunker complex connected by tunnels and ditches opposite their positions. He and his men could not find cover in order to get him. The young officer told me that the Gooks had rocket grenades and machine guns, and they were throwing everything they had at his men.

The Air Cavalry Mobile (armed helicopter squadron commanded by Major "Doc" Bahnsen call sign Thunderhorse 6), radioed me that they were on the way to help. As they neared the area, Thunderhorse 6 instructed me to line up my tanks and move forward, staying between the enemy bunkers and the American infantry platoon maneuvering behind the tanks. They would help clear the bunkers after our tanks crushed them. I talked with my platoon sergeant, John Kisner, to coordinate the move. I directed my driver to slowly head forward toward the bunker area. As we moved left, there was a yellow flash just a few feet from my face as my tank was hit.

I immediately dropped down into my turret. I later learned that four of my five tanks were hit by rocket propelled grenades (RPGs) when the infantry did not immediately follow the tanks, thus allowing the enemy to leave their bunkers and fire upon the tanks. Several tanks were on fire, but my crews escaped from the tanks although many were wounded. I couldn't see anything and was in pain but did not think about the extent of my injuries. I alerted the other tank commanders in my platoon by radio and feared that this might be the end for me. I was scared but able to regroup and focus on trying to be of some help. I told the air cavalry commander that I could shoot if he saw that I was aimed in the right direction. He told me to stay off the net and listen for my call sign "26" and shoot when I heard it. I heard my call sign and fired my main gun which was loaded with canister pellets. Suddenly, I was slammed forward against the turret as my tank came to a jolting stop. I must have been knocked out, since I did not hear the battle raging around me. The next thing I knew, I was being taken out of my tank by my crew and laid on the ground on a downhill slope below the rim of a bomb crater. I heard the noise of several helicopters circling the area and the occasional chatter of machine guns, along with the heavy smell of burnt gunpowder.

I began to realize I was hurt badly as I felt a large bandage across my eyes. My crew loader stayed with me until the fighting tapered off, and other men came for me with a stretcher. It flashed through my mind that, at age 23, this war and my Army career could very well be over. The bigger questions were simple: Would I survive my injuries, and if so, would I ever see again; or would the last image I saw be one of tanks, soldiers, dirt and jungle, and a bright yellow flash before blackness?

Later that day, I awoke in a field hospital at Bien Hoa. An Army nurse was at my side stroking my arm and telling me that I had just come out of surgery to have shrapnel removed from my eyes and other parts of my face. My head was covered with bandages. My left hand was also bandaged over my middle finger, which was stitched with wire and left open to heal. It was sliced opened from my middle knuckle to my palm.

The nurse assured me I would be ok. I stayed in this facility for about two weeks awaiting medical evacuation orders. A Vietnamese nursing assistant cleaned my wounds daily and changed the bandages. Since I could not see or use my left hand, she assisted me with meals by feeding me. Fortunately, or not, as the case may be, my intestinal track was stalled. That would become an issue soon.

The docs told me that they pulled pieces of metal from my eyes, and it would take a long time for them to heal enough for an evaluation by ophthalmologists to determine the extent of the damage.

Three days after the battle, Thunderhorse 6 showed up to visit me. He brought me a can of Bud in a paper bag and promised he would square it with the nurse as I downed my first beer in several days. He conveyed his regrets from Tyrant 6, Colonel George Patton IV, not being able to come himself, but told me that the Colonel was writing me a letter of appreciation for my service to the unit and the effort. He then relayed the results of the battle.

When all was said and done, 131 North Vietnamese regular troops were dead. What was thought to be a small unit turned out to be part of a large enemy company. They were survivors of the B52 raid the night before, and they had come out of Cambodia to the rubber plantation with heavy weapons and satchel charges. My tank platoon and the ground unit we assisted, along with air support from Thunderhorse 6, Major Bahnsen and his ground commander, Bengal 6 with his choppers, who took charge after I was out of commission, subdued and killed all enemy soldiers. Tyrant 6 (Patton himself) was hovering high above the action and observing his units in battle.

I learned later that my tank had rolled into a bomb crater and was out of the fight. Once the enemy was neutralized, troopers climbed onto my tank and extracted me. I remained protected in the crater until the dust off chopper arrived to take me to a more secure landing zone for medivac to a field hospital. Ironically, the dust off chopper was flown by Skip Munson, the pilot who rode in my tank for a day in the bush about two weeks earlier. Thus, March 20, 1969, ended with injuries to me, some of my men, and several infantry casualties. The enemy sustained huge losses.

My injury was the most significant in my platoon. Unfortunately, several of my troops were wounded, but none were as critical as mine. Major Bahnsen told me that my war was over, and I would be going home to recover. He wished me well and told me that he was putting me in for a combat medal. I thanked him, and I told him I was so proud to be a fighter with the Blackhorse Troopers. I also told him how much I wanted a career in the Army, but now it looked like that option was in doubt.

After about two weeks, my condition stabilized, and it was time to leave the field hospital and Vietnam. A jeep ambulance drove me to the main air base in Saigon for my flight on an Air Force hospital plane to Camp Zama, Japan, an army installation near Tokyo.

1

—

Growing Up

It was late summer of 1945. The Japanese Emperor and his staff would soon be boarding the battleship *USS Missouri* to surrender to America's General Douglas MacArthur. Officially World War II was over. Shortly before that happened, however, I was born in Gloversville, New York, to Michael and Mary Ann Szumowski. Mom was discharged from her Army nursing duties a few months before my birth, but Dad could not leave Europe and his Army Division until several months after my birth. I was the first grandchild of Frank Szumowski, the patriarch of our family, who, at the age of 14 and without much more than the clothes on his back and a couple of dollars in his pocket, emigrated from Poland through Ellis Island to start his life in America.

I was a 10-pound bundle of joy, or so I was told by my Mother. We know that Moms usually don't lie, but I suspect she had her moments of doubt during some teen escapades. I was the oldest of what would eventually be four boys born to Mike and Mary Ann. As I write this memoir, all brothers are alive and well with children of their own.

My earliest recollections of living in Gloversville, New York, are of happy times. The war had ended and my parents wanted to forget the war. They were eager to start a family and begin a happier life. They had survived the depression and the war. The first home I can remember was on Spring Street in Gloversville. We lived downstairs and an elderly couple with a son lived in the upstairs flat.

My father joined his brother and father in the family window cleaning business. My Mother was an Army nurse, and she continued a nursing career throughout her adult life.

Three years following my birth, my brother Rich came along, with brother Steve following 11 months later. So, the Spring Street home soon was chaotic with active boys.

Gloversville was a glove town, thus the name. It seemed like everywhere there was a leather mill or some aspect of the leather industry. I later learned that Gloversville was well known on the east coast for its fine quality leather goods: gloves; hand bags; wallets; baseball gloves; and other assorted leather goods. These were the post war years, and people had jobs, even if the pay scales were limited. Wages were usually enough for a family to afford a modest home or rent one at a reasonable price.

This was my hometown, where some 25,000 people lived, played, worked, went to school and worshiped freely.

Our neighborhood was comprised of solid, salt-of-the-earth working-class families of various nationalities. Most homes were two stories. Two families lived in each house. All neighbors knew each other and generally got along well.

Families were not rich in the material sense, but we all had pride and possessed what we could afford. The children grew up, went to school, and played in the neighborhood.

I remember getting my first Daisy air rifle BB gun. I was probably 10 years old. Dad taught me the proper way to handle this rifle.

I used to take my rifle and tube of BBs and sit on the ledge of my back yard to shoot at apples in our apple tree, the telephone pole in the neighbor's yard, practice hip shots at the two inch diameter clothes line pole and listen for the ping when it was a hit.

In later years, I graduated to using hunting rifles. I hunted deer with my Dad and Grandfather during deer season. I only saw one buck to shoot at and did. I thought I missed, but other hunters found the deer nearby gasping for breath. That incident affected me profoundly, and I never went hunting again.

When the hunters found the deer I shot and told me, I wondered how long it suffered and endured the pain before finally dying. I felt that hunting should be a quick death for the animal if you were going to hunt. That was my first opportunity to give any thought to killing animals for sport. Sure, we ate deer meat, but I was still troubled by the incident. Somehow, fishing was different for me. I caught fish, and they died, too, but they also became our dinner.

Fishing was a pastime I did enjoy. My brothers and I had many outings with Dad at nearby lakes and streams. My cousin Nestor and I fished together often after we were both old enough to drive a car. Those were fun times, and he and I bonded as he lived next door and was just a year younger than I.

My elementary school years were fun. It was there that I started to develop a liking for sports. Then kickball, dodgeball, monkey bar climbing, etc. were not frowned upon as they are today. The street kids would play wiffle ball, tackle football without equipment and other rough and tumble games that would make today's overly protective parents faint.

I don't recall too many serious injuries from sports activities, however I nearly put out an eye when I mistakenly let go of the stick tied to a rubber band which was notched into a groove on the underside of a handheld wood glider. When I pulled the glider back to stretch the rubber band, I let go of the stick and the stick flew up and hit my left eye.

I think my scream brought out half the neighbors. Fortunately, I did not lose my eye, but I scarred the iris and my vision went to 20/40 in that eye, and I required reading glasses thereafter.

Graduating from 6th grade was a rite of passage. Now, I would be walking eight blocks to the junior high school in the downtown area of Gloversville. This is where the subject matter was harder, although more interesting, to my developing mind. I studied the typical subjects for the middle school years. I learned that I had an ear for languages, so I excelled In French class and became fairly fluent early.

In addition to history, English, and science classes, I took shop class and enjoyed working with tools. This was not new to me. My dad had a workbench in our basement with lots of tools. I learned to use most of them. I started with a jig saw and made various objects out of soft wood. I later learned to use his band saw safely. So, I was at home in shop.

It was in the eighth grade that I became interested in basketball. My Dad installed a backboard and hoop on the side of our house in the driveway. I would spend hours shooting baskets during good weather. I can only imagine how irritating the clang of the ball on the rim must have been to not only Mom, but to the elderly couple upstairs. I was not tall enough to jump to the net to dislodge the ball when it was stuck in a wet net, so I had to stand on the capped oil pipe against the house to reach the ball. I was just a kid having fun.

I was in ninth grade when I began to realize I would be an avid sports fan, even if my own lack of skill in most sports meant I would be more of a fan than a participant. I showed interest in baseball, and my next door neighbor Buster, an independent driver for leather mills, decided he would buy me a baseball glove. The glove had Mickey Mantle's signature on it. He was my hero. I played American Legion baseball for several years as an outfielder, but basketball was my first love. Often we bear the scars of youth from crazy activities. Mine came during a baseball game when I foolishly stood behind the catcher without the benefit of a backstop between us. The batter fouled back a pitch that hit me squarely in the nose. My deviated septum is a reminder of that mistake so long ago.

The ninth grade also brought a surprise to our family. I was 13 years old and, in March, my youngest brother Tim was born. Being the oldest entailed some new obligations for me at times.

With two working parents, I would often take on babysitting duties, including diaper changes, bathing Tim, playing with him, and getting dinner started from the instruction list Mom left on the table. I attempted to herd my other brothers into helping out by setting the dinner table or taking over watching Tim while I fixed dinner. Mom usually worked the 3-11 p.m. shift at the hospital, so she was not often around for dinner except on weekends.

As we got older, the chores were split three ways. I usually cooked, and the table setting and dish clearing chores were done by Steve and Rich. Dad usually did the dishes after dinner and took time to read the paper. He would then descend to the basement to work on the project of the moment.

I enjoyed my time with Tim in his early years. He was fun and inquisitive. He and I had a special emotional bond that I knew I would miss when it was time for me to go to college.

Our family bonds extended beyond the immediate family. We were close with our aunts, uncles and cousins who lived in the area. Mom's mother and Dad's father and step-mother lived nearby also. We would gather during the summer at nearby campsites for picnics, swimming, and storytelling.

Christmas at our house was always exciting. We put up a tree, decorated it and always found many presents on Christmas morning. Stockings with our names were hung on a cardboard-cutout fireplace, and they would be stuffed with goodies that kept our dentist in business. We never lacked for fun gifts or the necessities for home and school. Mom and Dad worked very hard and sacrificed mightily for us. They were loving and caring, and our needs came before theirs.

Pop and Granny always hosted Christmas Eve at the farm. All of the Szumowski relatives would converge to feast on a polish tradition of pierogi.

The men and boys arrived in the late afternoon to have dinner. The kids would eat at the kitchen table. My cousin Paula was the table queen, as she was the only girl cousin until her sister came along. The adults sat at the dining room table. The kids always tried to outdo one another to see who could eat the most pierogis. I think I had the record of 14 one year. I still eat them but not in that quantity anymore.

After dinner, everyone would gather for Santa to pass out gifts. Soon, there were too many relatives involved for multiple gifts each, and we drew names for future gift-giving.

We loved those holiday times at the farm. It was always cold and snowy. It was a time of family reunions, sharing, caring about each other, and being reminded that Christmas was not about presents but about family and the birth of Jesus. Most of us went to mass at midnight and then went home to set out milk and cookies for Santa.

Easter was a similar family gathering, and our family usually hosted Easter dinner for Pop, Granny, Mom as my mother's mother was known, and my mother's brother Richard, who would occasionally visit us from Virginia. He usually made a trip to see us at Christmas, too. He was a wonderful person who was always there for us when things got financially stressful, and Mom asked him for help.

Years later, when I finished college and I was waiting to enter the army, Uncle Richard came to my financial assistance to help me repay the sales company I worked for after college. I took a draw against future sales of vacuum cleaners, then china dishes, pots and pans — all of which never materialized. Richard paid them off, and I repaid him over time from my army pay. That lesson in seeing his generosity and trust in my repayment has stuck with me to this day. I have helped my brothers, nieces and nephews as they have needed help. Fortunately, I am in a position to give them the help they need, rather than quibble about repayment. It brings me joy to do for them what others have done for me.

My high school years were fairly typical for the post war generation in Gloversville. We took classes and played sports. If you were good enough, you played for the school team; if not, you got involved with the YMCA basketball league, which was about the right place for my limited talents. We also joined school activities and clubs, went to sports games and cheered on our classmates. Some of us began to get interested in the opposite sex.

Call me a late bloomer, but I was not very interested in dating girls. I was probably 15 years old. Since I only had brothers, and I did not know much about girls. My mother made me enroll in a dance class one night a week. I had to wear a tie and sport coat. There were several of us with two left feet, so I didn't feel alone. The girls were also part of the class.

Miss Flint was the dance instructor, and she patiently walked us through the cha cha, waltz, foxtrot, rumba, and other dances few practiced today. The jitterbug was something we all enjoyed dancing. I learned the proper way to ask a girl to dance, how to hold her in my arms, and where to place my hand on her back while holding a clean handkerchief so I did not sweat on her dress. This all sounds so hokey now. I think it is the only time in my life when I actually used a handkerchief in that way when dancing with a woman. The night always ended with musical chairs, and the couple left standing each won a one dollar bill. In later years, those dance lessons came in handy.

I was a sports fan and religiously followed the Yankees, New York Giants football team and the Boston Celtics basketball team. My friends and I would argue over which player was the best center fielder. Mantle, Snider or Mays, but we all loved the Celtics during the Bill Russell era.

Most young people of my generation learned the value of family responsibilities and as we matured into adolescence. I remember dinner discussions between Mom and Dad about the election of Eisenhower as our President. Of course, "We like Ike" buttons were prominent in our house, but that is easily explained by virtue of the fact that Mom and Dad were World War II veterans serving during the war in France. That was also the beginning of lifelong Republican roots.

It was a time of tension in the world as America and Russia tested each other on the diplomatic front.

Family was important, and I don't recall anger or hostility in our family. I do remember tough financial times. We never lacked for food, clothing or necessities, but extras were absent during the lean times. We had a television, and I remember it being a big deal when we could afford a color television. The living room had a stand-alone radio console which included a turn table for Mom's 78 RPM records.

Dad and Uncle Nick would always go to Pop's farm on Friday nights to "check up." That was their term for counting up money and invoices for the week's work. As kids, we would often go to Pop's farm and play outside in nice weather. Pop had a garage with an attic loft that was a challenge to reach from a vertical ladder. There was also a barn with many areas for hiding and mischief. They had a chicken coop, and Granny, my Grandmother, would always warn us not to disturb them because they needed rest so they could lay eggs.

Granny and Pop had two dogs. Patch was a big friendly, gas-passing Dalmatian/Shepherd. They also had Rusty, who they called Puppy. He was a small Cocker Spaniel, and he was, originally, my first dog. We discovered that I had a dog allergy, so my grandparents took him to the farm, where he lived a fun life for a long time. I later took shots for various allergies. They cured me of most allergies, including dogs, and that would be fortunate for me as things turned out.

The farm was the gathering place for family reunions. Once a summer for many years, relatives from Amsterdam, Troy, Schenectady, and places downstate all came for a weekend of picnics, clambakes, corn-on-the-cob, burgers, hot dogs, and home-made dill pickles. Games included archery contests, softball games, horse shoes, and the opportunity to meet and get to know better near and distant relatives. Those fond memories stay with me today.

During my early teen years before I was old enough to get a legitimate job, I enjoyed spending winter nights reading, or making models of war ships, cars, and airplanes by patiently assembling them from the hundreds of little parts that needed to be glued in place. This was long before sniffing glue became the problem it was for future generations. They found various ways to get high on chemical substances. I also enjoyed collecting stamps and silver dimes. Too often, those dimes became Superman comic books, bubble gum and baseball cards, Milk Duds, Baby Ruth or Hershey bars, Dairy Queen ice cream cones and Coca Colas. I'd have been smart to hold on to my collections of dimes, comics, and baseball cards and spared myself the pain of dental fillings and weight gain. These were the times when I began to learn about focus, discipline and patience.

I took an interest in the Boy Scouts and was very proud of my uniform. The troop meetings taught me teamwork and discipline. Over several years, I earned many merit badges but did not stay with scouting long enough to become an Eagle Scout.

In my mid-teens, I tried my hand at being a caddy. I didn't get to carry many bags, but it was my first exposure to the game of golf. I caddied at the golf course where Jack Kobuskie, the high school basketball coach, played golf. He was a good golfer and later, when I was the team manager, he and I would sometimes talk about golf. He stressed the importance of patience, following the rules, integrity, and etiquette while playing the game. He believed in never playing fast and loose in any competition. He said, "You lose your integrity only once." He was a calm yet serious man. In two years of watching him, I never saw him angry about anything, especially during a game.

Winter brought different sport challenges. Tobogganing, skiing, snowball fights, and ice skating were fun winter activities for the neighborhood kids.

When the snowbanks were piled high for long stretches in the winter, we would dig tunnels through them and create intricate turns to foil anyone trying to come and find us. Today, parents who allow this activity would likely be prosecuted for child neglect, child abuse, or some such thing.

As I got older, shoveling snow was one of my chores at home, but it also became a money maker for me in the neighborhood. Many of the neighbors were older and unable to lift heavy snow. It may not sound like much now, but 50 cents to shovel a sidewalk was fine with me. I also earned money by mowing yards, washing cars, and delivering newspapers. There was not much work for someone under age 16 to do to earn spending money.

I would help my Dad in his window washing business as I grew older. This was hard work. Ladders were heavy, and your hands were always in water. My first tasks were always to wash screens in the spring and store storm windows in the basements of the homes where we worked. The windows were heavy, and this was the beginning of my upper body development. I enjoyed working with Dad, my Uncle Nick and my grandfather, Pop. This gave me some much needed spending money, as I was now approaching the age when I could drive. Dad and Mom were generous with their car when they did not need it, but I had to buy gas. Back then, it was a whopping 18 cents a gallon, and a buck bought a lot of gas.

My high school activities were varied. I joined the Key Club, and we did civic projects.

My primary activity in high school was to be a manager of the high school basketball team. I did that my last two years. I was nearly 6 feet tall, and the coach would occasionally allow me to dress and play in practice to help fill out a defense team when we were short of players. Those were fun times for me, and I gained some measure of respect from the team as someone who was more than just a ball-feeder for their layups, a trunk carrier for their warmup uniforms, and a supplier of orange wedges at halftime during games.

Those are fond memories for me. I eventually got the job of being the time-keeper during home games, and there I learned about attentiveness, responsibility for accuracy and rules to detail from the referees regarding time-keeping. I also learned patience when opposing coaches yelled about perceived mistakes on the time clock. Of course, a 17 year old was not about to get into a battle with an elder.

My basketball prowess, such as it was, was limited to Saturday mornings and afternoons at the YMCA. There was a league, and my final two years of high school would find me at The Y in the winter playing ball all day.

I did not have a girlfriend in high school. I would go to the school dances and stand with all the guys on one side of the gym and eye the girls standing on the other side of the gym. Records were playing music, and some girls would dance together until someone broke the ice and either cut in on them or slowly wandered over to the cluster of girls and got up the nerve to ask one to dance. Dating in high school was not a high priority for me. That would change when I went to college.

I recall our home life during high school as that of a loving, God fearing, respectful and hardworking family.

One summer, we went on a great outdoor trip. Dad, my Uncle Frank who was home for a while from his Air Force assignment, my two brothers Rich and Steve, cousin Nestor and I took a river trip. We had two canoes, and we ventured north to Tupper Lake region of New York State. We packed camping gear, food and water, and the six of us canoed down the Racquet River over several days. We camped on the river and swam as Dad and Uncle Frank cooked burgers, hot dogs and baked potatoes over hot coals. I remember Nestor and I had to hoist one heavy wooden canoe over our heads as we carried it overland to avoid a run of rapids and a waterfall. We arrived at Tupper Lake, and Mom and Aunt Jo waited with two cars to take us all home. That was a wonderful bonding experience for a teenager. I learned about water and boating safety, appreciated nature and the beauty of the wilderness, accepted young adult responsibility, learned a bit about wilderness survival, and began to understand teamwork and shared goals.

I was raised a Catholic, although my Mom was a Protestant. As was the practice then, and perhaps still, Mom agreed to raise her children Catholic. My brothers and I attended public schools, but when the time came for religious instruction, we went to church school at St. Mary's Catholic Church in downtown Gloversville. Nearly every Friday afternoon, the Catholic kids were "released" to walk the several blocks to their respective church school.

I went through various sacramental stages of the church and attended Sunday Mass regularly. As I matured into young adulthood, I often questioned the reasoning behind confessions. I knew that confessing sins was good for the soul, and God would forgive my sins. When I went to college, formal religion and I took a vacation from each other. It would be years later when I reconnected with my religious beliefs and rebuilt my spiritual foundation.

I learned the value of work with my first real job. I worked on weekends for a neighborhood general market. I was 16 and could drive, so I got to stock shelves, clean and sweep, help lift sides of beef onto weighing hooks, or placing meat slabs onto band saws for sectioning. I took an interest in the butcher trade and learned a lot about meat. I gradually got to wait on customers and learned valuable social skills interacting with customers.

The fun part of the job was putting orders for delivery together and then delivering them. I recall with a chuckle now, the first time the boss gave me the keys to his Chevy Bellaire for my first delivery run. Al said, "David, don't crash the car if you can help it." I loaded the trunk and hopped in the driver's seat and stared. It was a stick shift, and I had never driven one before. I knew the basics from watching Dad drive the truck. Somehow I managed to find the gears in the right sequence after some grinding, bucking and stalling. Once I got the hang of it, I preferred standard shifts, and my first two cars had it.

I saved most of my earnings from the market job as I was about to go off to college. The choice of college was simple in the end. I went where I was accepted. I had thought about West Point but had no connections to get in, and I was not good in the sciences. I had an uncle living in Richmond, Virginia, and our family visited him many times as we grew up. Vacations with him were often the only kind of vacation we could afford. We had fun times at his places in Virginia over the years. His last home was in southeast Virginia on Mob Jack Bay, a small bay off the nearby Chesapeake Bay. We would catch crabs, make crab cakes, swim in the bay, learn how to play canasta, and enjoy his small inboard yacht.

Richmond also had a quality private university which Mom's other brother Stuart attended in the post war years. So, I applied and was accepted. I began in the fall of 1963.

Much happened in America and the world as I finished high school. The Russians put Sputnik into orbit, the space race with Russia had begun with the goal of putting a man on the moon, Nixon lost to John Kennedy for the Presidency in 1960, the country botched the Cuban Bay of Pigs invasion, missiles were discovered in Cuba, we were on the brink of war with Russia over them, and I was graduating from high school.

My parents and grandparents attended my graduation. I was in the top 20% of my class, and my grandfather was especially proud as his first grandson finished high school. I was only a year older than he was at the time he courageously left his homeland to seek a better life.

2

College Years

It was the late summer of 1963 when Mom, Dad, and Tim brought me 500 miles south of Gloversville to start college at the University of Richmond. We arrived on campus and eventually found my dorm assignment. As it turned out, I had a single room overlooking the Student Center and Post Office. I met my floor mates and got the lay of the land using the map issued to new students. Mom and Dad spent a good part of the day with me, we hugged goodbye, and they went to visit Mom's brother before starting the long drive home. I registered for freshmen classes and began to live the college life.

I was a good student that first year. I took required courses and knew that the sciences would not be my major. Eventually, I settled on history and political science. The one selection of an elective that had meaning for me was Army ROTC.

Vietnam was heating up. President Kennedy sent Green Berets to Vietnam. I thought ROTC was a way to be patriotic. I enjoyed all aspects of the course, including weekly drill when I had to be spit and polished in my uniform. I was proud to be part of the ROTC Cadet Corps. I was always squared away when in uniform.

College also introduced me to the fraternity system. All fraternities had Rush Week, and I checked out several. I went to Phi Kappa Sigma, met some very nice guys, and made some early friends with others also rushing that fraternity. I chose it, and they pledged me.

Richard Sinclair was in the pledge class with me, and we became friends. We also decided to room together in our sophomore year. That fall, much changed in America. On a Friday in November, I was at the fraternity lodge with a few of the pledges. I was buffing the floor after the wax dried. The television was on, and Walter Cronkite interrupted the program to alert the nation that President Kennedy had been shot in Dallas. The buffer stopped, as did most activity in America. The campus was in shock and came to a standstill for the weekend. For most of us, this was the first hint of tragedy in our lives. It was also the harbinger of great cultural changes that were about to hit the 1960s. We were young but would grow up fast.

I studied, took exams, passed them, and the year flew past. Richard and I were inducted into Phi Kappa Sigma in the spring, along with seven or eight other pledges. Now we were lifelong brothers, secret handshake and all. As the next four years unfolded, many more Phi Kaps joined the brotherhood, and, to this day, a great many stay in touch with each other and remain very good friends.

Holidays were family time, and a Phi Kap named Dick Peterson and I became friends. He lived in northern New Jersey and had a car. He would give me a ride to his home where I would catch a bus to Albany, and my parents would pick me up. Over two years, Dick and I made many of these trips back and forth during school breaks.

My first summer home from college was one for a different type of work. The little market could not keep me full time, so I was able to land a job with the local school district maintenance department. I was a painter. I had experience painting, as Dad and I painted our house about three times over the years before I went to college. So, my summer was filled with work painting school rooms and stairwells. I would help Dad, Uncle Nick and Pop wash windows on Saturdays, go out to nightclubs several nights a week with buddies from high school, and generally try to stay out of mischief while having fun.

Soon, summer ended, and it was back to Richmond. Sinclair and I shared a ground floor room in one of the newer dorms. We were both fairly serious students. As the year went on though, I let my studies slip a bit. I was a solid B student, but my sophomore year found a few Cs and Ds on my first report. I spent too much time at the fraternity lodge, watched too much TV, and played too much ping pong. I was easily drawn away from studying to attend parties, go on dates, and get into other mischief. The only class I really enjoyed was ROTC and the drills and military history.

My sophomore year ended badly for me, and I was told not to return in the fall. I found a local job with the Bond bread company in Richmond. I would be loading a truck with bread, cookies, cakes and pies and driving about 60 miles to parts of rural Virginia to sell goods to the locals. I did this for about a week and thought it would be ok for a while.

Fortunately for me, the Dean of Students was a Phi Kap brother himself. Dean Robert Smart contacted my parents to talk with me. I was in Richmond, so my Mom called to tell me to contact the Dean. I did, and he wanted to see me.

Dean Smart met with me in his office and told me that my college career could be salvaged if I wanted to take two classes in summer school and pass with B's or better. I accepted and gave notice to Bond bread that I was returning to school.

I lived in my Uncle Richard's home in Richmond that summer and went back to school. I rode the bus to school and took economics and accounting classes. I met some students who lived near me. They gave me rides to the campus thereafter. I also got to know another student named Emmett Morgan, and he also lived near my uncle. Occasionally, I would ride with him also. He pledged my fraternity in the fall. We have been lifelong friends to this day.

That summer was fun, but I did not lose sight of the primary goal of studying. I got A's in my classes and was readmitted to college. Had this break not come along for me, I may have been drafted into the service.

I lost my opportunity to live on campus, but Dean Smart's secretary put me in touch with a friend who had a room to rent. She lived some distance from the campus, and I did not have a car, but the main road to school was well traveled by students and faculty. I would hitchhike and, more often than not, the ROTC Sgt. Major would pick me up and give me a ride right to the ROTC building.

My junior year was more focused, and my grades were much more in line with my first year. I became pledge master in the fraternity and focused more on studies as I matured. I played inter-fraternity sports, and began to take ROTC seriously, as now I had made a commitment to serve two years in the Army after graduation. Also, the Army was now paying me $50 a month.

I went home for Thanksgiving with my parents that year. To my surprise, Dad had managed to find me a car. It was an MG Sedan, grayish purple in color, with four doors, a stick shift on the floor and a radio. I loved that car and drove it back to college. Now I would not have to hitchhike to school.

The car had mechanical issues, so on spring break, I drove home and thought about a newer car. That was the year of the cougar. I saw the Mercury Cougar on the showroom floor, and it cost $2500. I borrowed money from the bank and bought it. My ROTC stipend would cover the monthly payment. I drove it to college, and it was my dream car. When I went to Vietnam, I turned the keys and payment book over to my brother Rich.

The summer of 1966 found me at Fort Indiantown Gap, Pennsylvania, which was where ROTC cadets from the eastern United States trained in summer camp. This was my first real experience with what Army life would entail. We drilled in all weather, did PT, shot pistols and rifles, learned small unit tactics, had chances to lead units, and learned teamwork. I graduated from summer camp ranked in the middle of my platoon.

My senior year consisted of finishing my course work in history and political science, writing a thesis on the history of the ROTC program at my university, and working the part-time job I had with the Richmond Post Office doing foot carrier mail collection. That job paid well, and it kept me with gas for the car, spending money, and the start of a savings plan.

I was a Dean's List student and had the highest GPA in the ROTC program. That, coupled with my summer camp standing, got me accepted into the Scabbard & Blade Honorary Military Society. Later I was awarded the Distinguished Military Graduate honor. That meant I would be granted my first choice of branch of service upon entry into the Army. I chose the Armor branch as I began to think about a career in the Army and knew that a combat branch would be the path to promotion.

I graduated in June of 1967 on the day of the Six Day War between Egypt and Israel. I was also commissioned as a 2nd Lieutenant that day. I would report to Fort Knox, Kentucky, for Armor Basic training in early January 1968.

I returned to Gloversville after college and helped Dad wash windows during the day and had odd jobs at a nearby resort at night. However, my real friends were in Richmond, so I returned to that area and lived with a fraternity brother and looked for work until I had to report to Fort Knox. I tried my hand at selling vacuum cleaners, fine china, pots and pans and silverware. I learned that I was not a very good salesman. My Uncle Richard's close friend lost his driver's license due to driving under the influence of alcohol. His job required travel, so I became his driver and that pay met my expenses. I reflected on his situation and what it cost him. I realized that there were several occasions during my latter college years where I exercised poor judgment by being behind the wheel after drinking. Fortunately, I was never stopped nor involved in an accident.

I went home for Christmas with my family before packing the car for my drive to Fort Knox, Kentucky, to serve my country. I never dated anyone too seriously while in college, so my leaving Richmond for Army service was not emotional. It would be eight years before a true meaningful relationship with a woman developed.

3

Patriotic Duty

I arrived at Fort Knox, Kentucky, on January 3, 1968, after two days of driving my Cougar from Gloversville. During the drive, I listened to the radio and had time to think about the new experience I was about to undertake. I had not given much thought to the rightness or wrongness of the Vietnam War. I grew up as the child of veterans. I understood love of country and service to her. I felt it was my duty to answer the call, and ROTC was the path I chose.

Americans were beginning to express themselves about the war on college campuses and in the media. Many thousands of Americans were dead or injured due to the war. I knew that I would likely be sent to Vietnam, since I was assigned to a combat branch of service. I resigned myself to the fact that it was a necessary step to take if I wanted a career in the Army. The thought of getting killed or injured was not one I dwelled on. I wanted to learn how to be an effective soldier and do my duty to the best of my ability. The career advancement would either happen or it wouldn't. It would be years later when I would reflect on the wisdom gained from experience and to apply critical thinking to the decisions of politicians and their definition of "best interests of America." The generation that grew up and lived through the Vietnam War no longer swallowed the government line on all issues. Much later in life, I became very cynical of the government and politicians. Neither ranked very high on the trust meter.

It was cold and snowy when I checked in to AOB (Armored Officer Basic) headquarters. I presented my orders and got directions to my barracks room in the BOQ (Bachelor Officer Quarters). The map of Fort Knox was part of a packet of materials I received, with the schedule of training and the various locations were also included. I found the officer's mess hall, ate and then went to my BOQ and unpacked.

Basic training was a twelve week program during which our class of about 100 young officers would learn how to lead tank platoons and armored cavalry squadrons. The training was rigorous, and the cold weather didn't help. To this day, the smell of diesel fuel makes me think of the exhaust fumes coming off tanks.

We learned map reading, leadership skills, gunnery skills, tank mechanics, weapons safety, unit tactics, and all the things a young officer needs to know to effectively lead soldiers and avoid career-ending mistakes. This included many war games where each officer had an opportunity to lead a mission in the field under war conditions.

I lived in the BOQ for the duration of basic school. The barracks were sufficient and each officer had his own furnished room. Training started early each day with fitness routines outside, if the weather was reasonably decent for winter in Kentucky, or inside if necessary. We were usually trucked everywhere for specific training subjects. While classroom work was significant, there were many subjects that required hands on training with weapons for firing qualification, tank mechanics, and map reading courses. Training was in daylight for the most part, but night exercises existed to present different challenges.

We were learning to be leaders of men in combat. The training tested our ability to absorb concepts, follow orders, and assume the awesome responsibility of carrying out a mission and taking care of the men who followed your orders.

The end of the course was highlighted by the Military Stakes run. This run was several miles with stations along the way to test our knowledge of all that we had learned in the course. There were about 30 different situations being tested. I would be timed on the Stakes run, but time stopped for each situation test. Once completed, the time started again on the run. I finished and passed. My new orders were to report to USATCA, the U.S. Training Center Armor command on Fort Knox. Many of my classmates were off to Germany or South Korea for duty, while still others were off to Jungle School in Panama for two weeks of intense training before further assignment to the war in Vietnam.

Fort Knox is a sprawling military Army base 40 miles south of Louisville, Kentucky. It has everything one would expect on a base that is home to armor units. The tank firing ranges were several miles from the base center. Some seasoned soldiers there told us that while firing the main guns, elevation was important since a miscue might have an artillery shell landing in some residential neighborhood; that, obviously, would not be good for the Army or the career of the officer making the mistake. My assignment was to be the Executive Officer of a tank training company for basic tank recruits in the training center. The company commander had the responsibility for training, and our Non-Commissioned Officers were in charge of the actual training.

The men learned to drive tanks, shoot machine guns and main tank guns, load weapons safely, set scopes to hit targets, change tank treads, fix engines, work as a unit and solve tactical problems. The men were graded on their performance and eventually went on to advance armor training. Advanced training usually meant they were going elsewhere in America or overseas.

I moved into a high rise apartment BOQ that bordered the post golf course. I had some old golf clubs with wooden shafts, and on my days off or after work in the late spring and summer, I would play golf with a couple of other officers and really developed a liking for the game. Social activity was somewhat limited. There were night clubs, and they were well-attended by local young ladies. Usually, I hung out at the Snake Pit, as the informal bar of the Officer's Club at the golf course was known. We tried to have fun but not get too serious as the future was uncertain.

I received orders transferring me that summer to temporarily serve in Pennsylvania at Indiantown Gap. This was the place of my college summer ROTC training, and now I would be going there as an instructor for about eight weeks.

I drove to the post and made contact with my Uncle Stu and his family in nearby Carlisle. I had a chance to visit them when I was a cadet, but now I was in charge of my free time. We had a few weekends together, and it was a good opportunity to get better acquainted with seldom seen family members.

My job that summer was to grade ROTC cadets as they were presented a specific field problem. This part of their training came at the end of their camp experience. The Colonel in charge told us to set up our problems. He then said he didn't want to see us for two weeks, and he didn't want to have to bail anyone out of jail.

A friend and I hung out together that summer and spent much of our spare time in Atlantic City, NJ. We would leave the Jersey Shore at 2 a.m. and drive like bats-out-of-hell and pull up at the training motor pool just as the truck was loading up officers for delivery to their respective field problems. One of us would change into uniform and use an electric shaver while the other drove to make us more or less presentable when we arrived. We would make a driver change stop quickly and the first driver would now shave and change. Our immediate supervisor, a Major, would look at us with a skeptical eye and inquire as to our sobriety. We assured him we were doing fine, albeit sleepy. The six weeks remaining flew past, and my summer break from tank training ended with a return to Fort Knox.

I continued Executive Officer duties and was also the Mess Officer and the Pay Officer. As Mess Officer, I mainly oversaw the Mess Sergeant's control and coordination of running the kitchen and supplying the food for our company. Actually, he did all the work, and I simply signed off on it. Feeding 150 men three times a day was a daunting task, especially when training required the troops to be in the field, and the food had to be trucked to their locations.

Once a month, I drew a .45 caliber pistol with ammunition and went to the payroll center to get the monthly pay for our trainees. I would sit at a table and count over $100,000 in various denominations and then fill each trainee's envelope with the exact cash he was to receive. I always counted twice to be sure. I then returned to my company area and guarded the cash until it was time for the men to lineup and get paid. Interestingly enough, my fraternity brother and good friend Emmett Morgan was stationed at Fort Knox, also. He was enlisted and worked in finance. I saw him now and then on base.

One weekend, I flew to Richmond to hang out with my college chums. Emmett was there, too, and he needed to go back to Fort Knox. He had his red VW bug, and I offered to ride back with him. We left Richmond and headed to Kentucky by way of West Virginia. The winter weather slowed us down, and we knew he would not be back on time. He was enlisted and had little flexibility with reporting back on time. We were approaching Charleston, West Virginia. We decided that he should catch a flight to Louisville, and I would drive his VW back to Fort Knox. I gave him my car key and told him to get my car at the Louisville airport and get back to base. He flew out, and I drove on through the night in a near blizzard. It took two days for us to get together to exchange cars. He enjoyed the salutes he got as various soldiers saw the officer sticker on my car and snapped off a salute to him. Of course, no one saluted me in his VW with the enlisted sticker.

My turn came to be Post Officer of the Day. This carried several duties. I needed to see that the post flag went up on time in the morning and came down on time at night. I was on call for any number of situations that might arise during a 24 hour period. At night, I needed to post sentries at strategic positions around the post, including Post Headquarters, the ammunition storage areas, the weapons depot, the tank yards, etc. At night, I would make my rounds to insure everyone was at their assigned post. At 5 p.m. daily, the OD, as the position was known, had to call a certain telephone number exactly on time to avoid what was known as an El Dorado alert. If the OD missed the timing by as little as two seconds, the alert was called and a truck of soldiers and a tank was sent immediately to the Gold Bullion Depository on Fort Knox. Everyone who had the OD assignment dreaded missing that call. We would watch the second hand on the HQ clock and dial 6 of the 7 numbers and hit the last digit one second before 5. I did it correctly.

A famous story went around that at one time, an officer had the duty and missed the call. He knew that he needed to proceed to the Gold Depository by the most direct route. So, taking that instruction literally, he climbed onto the tank and drove directly to the vault. Unfortunately for him, he ordered his tank driver to drive the 50 ton tank over the officer's golf course. The tank chewed up fairways and greens. Thereafter, all future alerts were directed to proceed by "direct paved" routes.

My time at Fort Knox was coming to an end. I received my orders to attend Jungle School in Panama in January of 1969 for two weeks, then have two weeks leave, before leaving Travis AFB in San Francisco for my trip to Vietnam.

Fort Sherman was the Army base in the Canal Zone. We arrived on an Air Force plane from Charleston, South Carolina, at Howard Air Force

Base, also in the Canal Zone. We were bused from the AFB on the Pacific side to Fort Sherman, on the Caribbean side. There, we were assigned barracks and double bunks for two weeks. Panama was hot in January. We learned about adjusting to heat, water rationing, being alert to safe and dangerous plants and animals, jungle foods, patrols, expectations in Vietnam's jungles, and small unit jungle tactics. We learned to rappel down steep terrain, do a rope slide across a river, and make a flotation device from elephant grass stuffed into our ponchos. The flotation device would carry our gear and, hopefully keep it dry. We also learned to swim against a river current to finish a mission. The two week process was physically taxing.

The final test of our endurance was an evasion course. We were set up in teams of four. We were dropped at a point and shown on the map where we were, and we were also shown where we had to go to finish without being captured by the enemy. We hit the jungle immediately and used our compass to determine the best way to move forward and avoid capture. This was raw jungle with all the critters one might imagine. We kept a constant vigil for snakes, spiders, iguana, vines, swamps, and the enemy. We did not want to be captured. If we were, we would get a taste of discomfort similar to what real capture by the enemy might be like. A poncho, machete, canteen, some C rations, and a compass were our tools of the trade for that day. We started at 6:00 in the morning and finished near 6:00 at night. Our group was about the fourth or fifth group in, and many groups spent the night in the jungle. We were tired, hungry, wet from rain and trudging through swamps, and itching from mosquito bites. Our self-confidence was very high. I had proven to myself that I could handle stress, and I was proud of my accomplishment.

The colonel in charge of the school awarded us certificates and gave us the next day and night off. We went into Colón, Panama, for a night of drinking and partying. We were careful to remember the bus schedule to return to the post for the departure of the buses to Howard AFB and the return flight to America. As we flew home, we all knew we were off to the war, and life for us was going to change. Sadly, it would change for some irrevocably.

I returned home to visit my parents. I spent a few days with them before saying goodbye and heading to San Francisco to meet up with

Richard Sinclair for our three final days in America before life got more challenging.

The TWA flight left Travis Air Force Base in the rain. I was buckled up at my window seat as one of about 175 other Army, Navy, Air Force and Marine men about to endure a 20 or so hour flight to the Republic of South Vietnam to join America's war effort. We would stop in Hawaii to take on fuel for the leg of the flight to Guam, where we would refuel again for the flight to Saigon, South Vietnam. This flight was unlike flights of today. We had only a book or magazine to read but no movies to watch.

Overseas flights were arduous, and the seasoned flight attendants, then known as stewardesses, were senior employees. They were skilled at small talk, fed us often, monitored alcohol intake if we were old enough to drink, and kept our spirits up because all of us knew that some would never be coming home again.

The pilot alerted us that we were skirting the coast of China as we flew south toward our destination. Most of the passengers had an instamatic Kodak camera, and soon the left side passengers were passing their cameras across the aisle to have seat mates take a photo of the Chinese coast off in the distance. It was nothing more than a mere smudge on the horizon.

I knew that photo would join the several that I took while on a final 3-day visit to San Francisco before leaving on this flight. My old college roommate, Richard Sinclair, met me in the city, and we hung out together seeking girls, bars, sites, and generally enjoying our last couple of days in America. Richard was scheduled to fly out on a later flight, the same day I left. We did cross paths again in Vietnam on our first full day there.

The Saigon landing approach was unlike any landing I had experienced. The plane made a speed descent, turning left and right and left again all at about a 45 degree angle. I looked at my seat mate with a questioning expression. He said it was a typical combat zone landing. It was to present a smaller glide path onto which enemy artillery could focus weapons to try to shoot us down. He said all landings and takeoffs in a war zone were steep. The plane leveled out and landed smoothly and quickly. My initial shock came at the door when stepping onto the stairs to deplane. The heat was as if standing in front of a blast furnace. Welcome to Vietnam in February 1969!

We departed the stairs angling right. To our immediate left was a long line of military personnel waiting to board the same plane. We were fresh and fairly presentable. They were hardened veterans of a year in Vietnam. These were men and women who aged quickly. Many wished us luck. Others chanted to "get Charlie," the slang term for the enemy. Others just looked at us with a vacant stare. Buses dropped us off at various unit depots for further reassignment pursuant to our orders.

Long Binh Junction (LBJ) depot was my first point of military contact. There, I was assigned a bunk, told where to eat, and also where to draw my gear. I was issued a steel helmet, jungle camouflaged fatigues, jungle web boots, socks, underwear, web gear, ammo pouch, canteen, and a .45 caliber pistol and ammunition. I turned in early as I was tired from the long flight.

I had the next day to rest and check out the depot. Richard Sinclair and I did see each other briefly that day, as he was routed through the depot to get his gear. We both got orders later that day and would be separating again in the morning. He would go north, and I would go south.

At 4 a.m., a corporal woke me and told me I had 30 minutes to get dressed, grab some chow and get my gear to the HQ for a short ride to the chopper pad at the 11th Armored Cavalry Regiment. I met the unit Executive Officer who informed me that I would be going to the Forward Base Camp at Xuan Loc to join up with my tank platoon. He told me that Colonel George S. Patton IV was the unit's Commanding Officer. As I left headquarters, I saw Colonel Patton's sleeping quarters. He had a standalone carriage similar to the one his father used in World War II and which was on display at the Patton Museum at Fort Knox. I grabbed my duffel bag and boarded a chopper for the flight to my new unit.

At Xuan Loc, I was met and escorted to my unit's staging area. I went to HQ to do the necessary paper work regarding my will, my pay, etc. There I saw a guy I knew from my basic training days at Fort Knox, Kentucky. I called to him by name. Oops, that was a mistake. He now outranked me. He came over with a not so friendly face to say hello and reminded me that this was not Fort Knox. I apologized, and we parted, never to see each other again. I thought he was a bit of a tight ass!

I had a bunk in a plywood shack surrounded by sandbags. I was quickly reminded that this war was my priority. At night, rifle fire at the perimeter reinforced that thought.

The next day, I observed the activity at the base. There were small fixed-wing planes bringing in troops and cargo. Helicopter squadrons flew in and out throughout the day. Tank units were being maintained in the motor pool area, while others left the base in convoy formation. I observed several Armored Personnel Carrier squadrons preparing for convoy escort duty also. I was driven by jeep out to where the company was set up for patrol operations. I met my company commander and got the lay of the land from him. He was from San Diego, California, and it is ironic that seven years later, I would find myself starting over in San Diego.

I was introduced to my platoon members. I was the leader of a 5-tank platoon, and I had an experienced platoon Sergeant to work with me and show me the ropes.

Each tank had a commander, driver, loader, and gunner. We ran routine patrols in III Corps around the Saigon area. Occasionally, we worked near and with the First Infantry Division. We got into one fire fight within a week of my arrival. Fortunately, we had no casualties from that engagement, and the Regimental CO flew out to inspect the area as we moved on toward a night secure position. My tank rolled past him as he stood next to his chopper, and there was no mistaking those pearl-handled revolvers on his hips. Colonel George S. Patton IV, son of the famous general of World War II fame, stood by his chopper with helmet in hand and nodded at me. As I passed, I started to salute. He shook his head as he waved me down. I should have known better than to try to salute an officer in the field when enemy soldiers would like nothing better than to know who was the boss and try to take him out. Of course, his personal helicopter would have told the enemy all it needed to know.

Patrols were routine, and we were always vigilant. We found a stream in which to swim. We set up a perimeter and took turns in group swims. We would toss a grenade into the water to kill leeches before taking our swim. After, we would check each other to insure that none of the critters attached to us.

At night, we would pull guard duty for four hours and focus our attention on the barbed wire which enclosed our company area. Trip flares were set nightly to alert us to enemy infiltration to the secure area.

There was always some enemy contact somewhere in the area. It was quite a show when Cobra gunships would arrive on the scene to fire a stream of thousands of bullets into suspected enemy positions. We always knew when Cobras were firing their Gatling gun because a giant ripping sound cut the air and made mulch of anything they struck.

On one routine patrol, I was assigned a chopper pilot from the air mobile squadron attached to the 11th Cavalry. The squadron had Huey gunships and light observation helicopters known as mosquitoes or LOHs. Skip Munson was the pilot riding with me as we patrolled. He wanted to get some sense of what it was like on the ground for the units he would assist from the air. I thought the idea was practical and being with me gave him a first-hand view from my perspective. We spent the day together and wished each other luck in the future. Little did we know that our paths would cross again very soon.

I learned that our company commander was in a helicopter accident and was being sent home. Our new commander took over and, within three days, he accompanied my platoon into an enemy engagement which resulted in shots being exchanged for a hectic five minutes. I felt a punch on my back near my shoulder. Thank God for my flak jacket. Later, I checked the area and saw the fabric torn. I'm assuming I was shot at but got lucky. We didn't find any enemy soldiers, but there was a cache of weapons, ammunition and rice that we confiscated. Just another day in "Nam."

I had been in Vietnam for slightly more than a month. The daily routine was usually not that eventful. We assisted other units providing heavy armor when they thought they needed it. We saw the results of fights of other units. The enemy did not always police their dead, so the surrounding area often had a stench of death. When not confronting hostile troops, our day consisted of maintaining our tanks and weapons, getting a hot meal, trying to stay clean standing buck naked in front of a tank with a gallon bag of water and spout hanging from the muzzle of the main gun for a shower, sleeping when we could, and writing letters and making tapes for loved ones. The air was filled with the smell of diesel fuel, grease, body odor at times, and the sound of radio music from the Army radio station. Each tank crew got to know each other well because we knew our teamwork was critical when things got hot.

It was March 19th. I noted that it would be my brother Steve's 20th birthday that day. Tim's 10th birthday would follow in two days. The next day, however, would bring something very different for me.

*For his bravery in combat, Szumowski
was awarded the Silver Star — the nation's
third highest award for valor;
the Bronze Star with "V" device and
oak leaf cluster; the Purple Heart;
and the Vietnam Service Medal with
two bronze service stars.*

———————— ☆ ————————

4

——

Flying Home

At Camp Zama, I spent about three weeks for rest and further eye evaluation by specialists. They removed stitches from my eyes, and I was able to walk with the help of hospital staff, since I could not see where I was going. Captain Marilyn Sylvester was the Charge Nurse for my ward, and she took great care of me. She was also a stickler for inquiring about my bowel habits. I still had not had a movement and, when it was going on 21 days, she said "Lieutenant, you will have a bowel movement today. You may have it on your terms, or you will have it on mine."

That did the trick, since I did not want to find out what her terms might be. Thereafter, I had no further intestinal issues.

Captain Sylvester was not one to let me simply lie in bed and sulk. She forced me to walk with her around the ward, helped me with letters to family and friends by doing the writing for me, and made sure I ate properly because I had lost considerable weight. I recall her taking me outside one spring day, and we strolled among the cherry trees so I could get some fresh air and smell the cherry blossoms. Her kindness and support kept me from falling into depression.

One morning, Captain Sylvester came to my bedside and said, "David, you will be leaving us tomorrow." She told me I would be flown by the Air Force on a hospital plane to Alaska and then on to Walter

Reed Army Hospital in Washington, DC. There, I would convalesce until the Army medically retired me.

The next day, dressed in hospital clothing, Captain Sylvester gave me a hug and wished me well. She gave me her mailing address and told me to let her know how things were going. For several years, we exchanged letters until we lost track of each other. Those letters of encouragement were a good support for me as I would struggle with the traumatic stress that was about to challenge my future.

After leaving Japan, we landed in Alaska and stayed long enough to refuel. Once airborne, the flight staff let me get up from a hospital bunk and move to a regular plane seat for the leg of the flight to St. Louis. There we deplaned for the night and stayed in barracks. The next morning, the flight brought us to Washington, DC. A bus took the injured Army soldiers from the plane to Walter Reed. This would be my home for nearly five months.

Back in Gloversville, the day of my injury was not the happiest day for my brother Steve and his birthday. The Army sent a telegram to my parents to inform them of my being wounded in Vietnam. The telegram was short on details and promised more news as it became available. My family took the news hard. Steve told me that Dad kept a map of Vietnam on the wall, and at this news, he ripped it down. I eventually got a letter off to them from Vietnam with the help of a nurse who wrote it for me. I told them that I could not see. This news devastated my mother, an Army nurse herself, who had seen so much tragedy during World War II in France.

In Japan, I was able to talk with my family using the Military Assistance Radio Service (MARS) with phone relays via short wave radio operators. The call was short in duration, but being able to hear my voice helped them immensely. They would visit me upon my return to Washington.

Washington, DC in the springtime was beautiful. The cherry blossoms were out, the weather was warm, and the nation was getting used to President Nixon's plan for the country and its extraction from Vietnam. The country was in turmoil about the war. It was a time of sex, drugs, and rock & roll. Free love was in the air, and I was in the hospital.

I was in a hospital ward with five other soldiers with eye injuries. My closest bunk buddy was Warrant Officer John Todd. He was a chopper pilot who was shot in the face while flying. He survived somehow, and he also learned that he was blind. He had lost feeling in his nose and most of his face. He was at Walter Reed before I arrived and was still there when I left at the end of August. We got to be good friends during our time together. We would reconnect years later and discover that we had both pursued a career in law.

Mom and Dad came to Washington, DC, to visit me shortly after my arrival. They brought Tim, too. He had just turned 10. I remember clearly when they entered the room. Tim ran to me and hugged me so hard I nearly choked. We were both crying, and I tried to tell him things would be okay. Mom came next with a big hug and tears. Dad was not emotional as a rule, but he was choked up as we shook hands. I remember him being similarly emotional when he saw me off at the airport not quite seven weeks earlier. He gave me a hug then and said, "Don't be a hero."

We had a nice visit for several days, and Mom made time to see Dr. Joe Shock, the ophthalmologist who was handling my treatment. Dr. Shock never sugar-coated his findings with us. He explained the extent of the damage to both of my eyes. I could see nothing, although I thought I had some light perception. Looking back on that time, I'm not sure that I really did see light.

Dr. Shock said that it would be several years before my eyes recovered from the trauma and to know if I would see again. In hindsight, I believe he was letting me down easy. One eye was shrunken badly and the other had extensive damage. He knew it was highly unlikely I would ever see again.

Plans were underway to medically retire me. In the meantime, I was given significant convalescent time. I went home for several weeks, visited with old friends and neighbors, and tried to not be a nuisance. Tim was in grade school at that time, and Rich and Steve were away at college.

I spent time with my grandparents, Mom's mother and especially Pop. He was alone now, having lost Granny the year before. We talked mostly of family, and I heard about his trek to America at the age of 16 with the clothes on his back and a few dollars in his pocket. When he came to America, he did not speak English and settled in northern New Jersey after clearing Ellis Island immigration in 1910. He married and had three children by the time he was 26. My Dad was one of those children, and he did not speak English until he was much older. Polish was the language of the house. I still have a tape of my talks with Pop about coming to America and having the tremendous opportunity to succeed here.

Home made me restless after about a month, so I returned to Walter Reed and became a bum while still in the Army. One day, a few of us in the "blind wing," as we called it, decided to pay a visit to "the Snake Pit." That was the name of the ward across the main hall. This ward held the soldiers with orthopedic injuries, and they were a rowdy bunch. Everyone in the ward was entitled to two beers a day. Somehow, those guys managed to get more, and the nurses called them incorrigible. We caned our way over to visit. There, with his busted up leg in traction, was Skip Munson. He did not know I was at Walter Reed, and I did not know he had been injured in a crash. We caught up, recalled our day together on the tank and his recollection of dusting me off from the battlefield to the chopper that flew me to the field hospital.

John Todd and I had a lot of fun with the nurses. We had student nurses tend to us for several months. He and I devised a scheme to get back rubs every day from each student nurse. Three rubs a day was heaven. We promised to pick a winner in a month, buy the winner a dozen roses and treat her to dinner at the Mess Hall of her choice. We figured the roses would be the expensive item. After one day of back rubs, we both knew who would win. The challenge was to keep it going for a month and keep the losers interested enough to think they had a shot.

I met some lady friends through fraternity brothers who came to visit. So occasionally I had a date out on the town. Having to return to the hospital was a damper on those evenings.

I also went back to Richmond to visit the University of Richmond campus and reconnect with friends. My last college girlfriend had moved on and seemed happy with the new guy in her life. I went to parties, had some dates, and just killed time waiting for my Army retirement.

Upon my return to Washington, I learned that the hospital commander was going to pin a Silver Star medal on me (see page 131). I had become a bum of sorts. I had let my hair grow and had sideburns. A young captain came to square me away for the ceremony and said, "Lieutenant, those sideburns have got to go. The ceremony will be covered by the hospital PR machine, and there is no way the Colonel will let you show up like that." With reluctance, I shaved them off. The ceremony was very nice, and I was standing tall and proud in pajamas and a bathrobe as I received my Silver Star, along with my Bronze Star for valor and a Purple Heart for my wounds. Several guys from the ward attended the ceremony. That night we got three beers!

One highlight of the stay in Washington was a trip on the Sequoia, the President's yacht. Injured soldiers and sailors from Walter Reed and the Bethesda Naval Hospital were given a long ride on the Potomac River and fed a nice lunch. We were escorted by volunteers and some dignitaries. I recall the daughter of the Secretary of Agriculture being attentive to those of us without sight.

One day while shooting the breeze with my ward mates, a familiar gravelly voice came from our doorway and asked to join us. I was a smoker then, and he asked to join us in a smoke. He was Senator Everett Dirksen of Illinois. He was in the hospital for a medical checkup but quietly wandered away from his room and his aide to steal a smoke. The hospital was in a panic — it seemed they had lost a U.S. Senator. The staff finally discovered him with us, and all was well. I recall him lamenting about the war that brought such heartache to so many families and our nation.

The summer of 1969 was tumultuous. The protests against the war continued. President Nixon was pursuing a peace settlement with the North Vietnamese which would also provide honor to the South Vietnamese. Rock & roll was in full swing in America. Protest songs abounded, and the college campus was alive with antiwar sentiment. Those of us at Walter Reed did not have much sympathy for the protesters and draft dodgers. We focused on things American. There was baseball, and the major accomplishment of an American landing on the moon.

I finally received the paperwork for my retirement. A representative of the Veterans Administration had visited me early in the summer to talk about my VA benefits and blind rehab. Russ Williams was himself blind, and the Chief of Blind Rehab within the VA system. I was going to be enrolled in their program at Hines VA center in Maywood, Illinois. It was August of 1969, and I said goodbye to John and my other friends in the blind ward. I went to the Chicago area for the 16-week rehab program that would teach me how to live without sight. I was nervous about the rehab program, but I was also ready to get on with my life.

5

New Skills

Maywood, Illinois, is a quiet little suburb located west of Chicago. Hines VA Hospital is the home of a huge complex of hospitals and clinics. It also housed the first blind rehabilitation center for soldiers, sailors, airmen and marines wounded and blinded in combat. The facility was started in the late 1940s when the VA realized that the military's Avon Old Farms Convalescent Home in Connecticut was inadequate for the number of blinded vets returning from World War II.

In late August of 1969, it was my turn to meet the challenge of their program. The blind rehab wing was inter-connected to the main hospital so that no one had to go outside to get from one wing to another. Of course, one could go outside, and much of my training was outside. I was sitting in my modestly furnished room on one corridor of the complex my first afternoon at the hospital. I heard a knock at the door and told whomever to come in.

"David," said someone, "My name is Frank Wood, and I am your mobility instructor. You can call me Woody." We shook hands. I sat on my bed, and he sat in the one chair in the room. He welcomed me to Hines. He knew of my background, my injuries and was warm, friendly and welcoming.

He told me about the program. It was a 16-week program, but there was no pressure to finish until I was ready. He reviewed the daily schedule with me which included "orientation" twice a day for an hour each. All classes were an hour. Other classes included braille, shop and daily living skills. Orientation was his area of expertise. In his class, I would learn to use a cane effectively and safely. In time, I would learn to navigate all of the different situations I would face once I left Hines.

He then took me on a sighted-guide tour of the entire wing and connection to the hospital and canteen area where I could buy cafeteria food items, small personal items, and just have a place to socialize. It was like a small diner and mini PX combined. We passed by the room where I would take my meals. It was about a five-minute walk from our wing to the chow hall.

The facility had several corridors with rooms for various classes. There was the administrative area, a laundry facility near a small gym for stationary bike workouts and weight lifting. We walked around for about thirty minutes with me holding his elbow. He showed me the initial techniques of walking with sighted help. We met other staff members and the head of the department, John Malamazian. I later learned that he was a legend in the blind rehab movement.

I was also shown the bathroom and shower facility available to my hall. I would be sharing the facility with seven other vets. The facility contained two showers, two stalls, two urinals and two sinks. It worked out fine.

Most of us were young Army vets. There were also a few Marines. I recall that I was the only officer in the program, and I was also the only one who had gone to college; however, here, in this place, we were all retired and similarly injured. We were all at various stages of training, and I tried to keep an open mind about training and making friends.

I was measured for a long cane and given one adjusted for my height. The first day after I arrived was a weekend day, so there was no training. I had a talking book machine (essentially a record player for recorded books on disks) in my room, and I had a radio. My wing had a library of recorded books, so I grabbed one. It was the beginning of my reading life without sight, and it has probably numbered over 5,000 books if not more. When you are blind, passing time in a constructive way is very important. Some of the guys slept the day away. Others went to the day room where there was a television, and it was football season. I read until it was chow time. Because I was new, an instructor escorted me to the cafeteria. He oriented me to the layout of the room and showed me how to find my assigned seat after going through the food line. He showed me how to hang my cane on the back of my shirt by its hooked end. So, I shuffled along with my tray in both hands and the long cane bouncing off my butt as I walked. The food was fairly decent for institutional food. It was a good thing too, since I was going to be here a while.

Woody met me at my room on the first day of training, and we got started with my rehab. I was a little nervous, but after five months of not doing much at Walter Reed, I was ready to learn. I first learned that I had bad cane habits from using it improperly while hospitalized. Woody showed me the proper way to hold the cane, and the proper swing arc while walking. It took a while for me to become comfortable with this new technique and confident enough to keep from hitting the wall with the cane as I walked. The cane arc and ground touch are always opposite the foot that is moving forward. Thus, when you take your next step, you will be stepping into the area you just safely cleared with the cane. Eventually, I got a rhythm going, and it worked well until I met an obstacle like a drinking fountain, a person walking slower than I was, or coming to a dead end. We spent about a week indoors working the corridors, connecting halls to other buildings, and identifying sounds and smells to help orient me to locations. This would all come in very handy later in the program and in my life.

Not many people have good spatial ability, but apparently I was someone who did. I could simply "feel" the air pressure change against my face when something was too near. I avoided many whacks to my head because of this ability, especially when encountering things pro-truding from a wall or hanging too low to clear without touching it. The change in sound from tapping and air pressure flows when passing open spaces worked to my benefit also. They helped me to adjust direction and find turns into corridors. Unfortunately, those abilities did not translate to things protruding at a lower level. It became imperative to use proper cane technique to avoid thumps to my shins.

The cane was also critical for detecting stairs. It was necessary to make sure the cane tapped the floor. My reflexes were fairly good, and as I got better with the cane, I walked faster. If I got careless and forgot to touch the floor, I could find myself taking a tumble and getting seriously injured. Believe me, falling up a staircase is preferable to falling down one. If you don't think sounds change, clap your hands together before entering a stairwell and then again just after entering. You will detect a significant change and learn, as I did, to be alert.

Another part of early training was discovering braille. Most of us are not sensitive with our fingers when it comes to feeling six dots individually with an index finger, especially when each raised dot is the size of a pinhead. I took braille lessons for a good portion of the training program, but I never would be proficient at it as life went on. I knew the basics of Grade 1 and Grade 2 braille, memorized the contractions and learned how to use a braille machine to write in braille. I knew I would never read a book in braille. It would take forever, and it would also take up a lot of space. Years after leaving Hines, I bought a pocket dictionary in braille. The print version fit in my shirt pocket. The braille version was the size of a magazine, about three inches wide and consisted of seven volumes. I never bought anything again in braille.

I took a typing class that was fairly easy, because I already knew how to type. However, the instructor insisted on putting me through the course her way with a manual typewriter using paper and carbon and ribbons. I bit my tongue as I did the lessons. Finally, I took the speed test and typed about 50 words a minute with no mistakes. Yeah, success! Now I was able to do more but with an electric typewriter. I'm sure I attempted many eye rolls, but since I wore dark glasses, no one knew if they rolled or not. The damage to them likely meant they did not.

Shop class was where I began to develop a touch of attitude. I was real handy with tools from my years at home with Dad and all of his tools. Nevertheless, my first shop project was to take several pieces of leather of varying sizes and make a wallet. Well, I had done this as a Cub Scout or Boy Scout or even just for something to do on winter nights at home. You have plastic string which we called gimp in the old days, you attached it to a needle and then weaved it in and out over a zillion holes in the leather.

I thought the whole exercise was stupid and insulting. Well, because of my attitude and feeling above it all, I did it incorrectly. Yep, the gimp was twisted, and I missed some alignment of holes. You guessed it, a do over. This was beginning to piss me off.

Since graduation to something more interesting would not occur until I mastered the dumb wallet, I exercised patience for a change and managed to do it correctly. This darned wallet took about a week to get right. The instructor in shop, Lee, asked me one day, "David, are you ready for something new and challenging?" He showed me to a seat, showed me a loom and told me I was going to make a rug.

I looked toward his voice and, before I could say anything, he handed me some yarn, a tool for sliding it through yarn strung into the loom, and he showed me the pedals and how to operate them. Okay, so this was going to require some thought and concentration if the pattern was going to come out correctly. I was damned if I was going to screw this up and have to do it twice. I didn't. So, I spent two weeks in shop, and a wallet and a rug were my gifts to myself. At least I used the rug on the floor near my bed.

You may recall that I was the main cook in our family as I was growing up because both of my parents were working. Because of that, daily living skills training was a total insult to my intelligence and skills. Come on now, I have cooked, baked and fried food, eaten C rations, and worked in a butcher store. I know something about daily living skills, especially in a kitchen.

Miss whatever her name was showed me the sink, gave me a pan and told me to put water in it. Are you kidding me? She hands me an egg, and she tells me we are going to make a hard-boiled egg. She brings me to the stove, shows me the burner dials, gives me a timer, shows me the markings and how to set it. I must have had a disgusted look on my face because she proceeded to lecture me on the importance of knowing how to safely maneuver around a kitchen where one could cause a gas leak, start a fire, cut oneself with a knife, or spill something — blah, blah, blah.

I tried to tell her about my experience, and she understood. She said it was all well and good, but I had not done it without sight. We were going to get through this and bake cookies, a cake, and cook a full dinner before

I would pass her course. The saving grace was that I could decide what that meal would be. I managed to do it with some flair.

It was now about three weeks into the program, and I was feeling good about my mobility work. We were getting outside and learning about Maywood. We would walk the streets, cross them safely, go into stores, shops and restaurants and learn how to move around in them safely. Balance is often difficult when one cannot see, so no one wants to be the "bull in the china shop." I was careful in stores where one misstep off a line could result in a shoulder or arm wiping out a shelf of items.

We learned how to find bus stops, get in and out of cars safely, and pay attention to details in various situations. Getting lost and figuring out how to find something familiar was part of the learning process. Before the program ended, we would be deliberately left in places we were unfamiliar with, and the final test of our skill and ability was to find our way home.

Shop class was becoming more interesting. I finished my rug and now got to graduate to something which I found to be more challenging. I was given preformed stool legs and had to weave strips of bamboo into a pattern to make a seat for this stool. That was fun and took about a week. Then I made a stool from scrap material. I used measuring tools, a saw, a miter box for angles, and screws and nuts for the holes. I drilled successfully, sanded and varnished the stool, and it became a fixture in my Mom's house. The final exercise in shop class was to make something using a lathe. I had never used one before, so my interest was piqued.

I started with a block of wood that was 6x6x2. I learned to find the center and lock it onto the lathe. Using a hand guard and chisels, I made the block of wood round. By changing the angle of approach with a chisel, I bowled out a ring about two inches wide, leaving a hump in the center of the wood. I then used a drill press to perfectly center drill a hole in the hump. This was the base of a lamp, and the electric cord would be fed through the hole.

I took another block of wood about 4x4x12 inches and centered both ends on the lathe. Using chisels, I shaped this wood into a cylinder and then further deepened grooves to give it a teardrop effect at either end. I spent hours sanding both pieces smooth using the lathe and holding sandpaper in my gloved hands. I used the drill press to put a hole into the length of the wood and varnished both pieces before fitting them together into a finished lamp. I was very proud of this project. I asked the instructor if I could make a second one just like it, and he allowed me to do it. I still have these lamps.

In hindsight, which is always 20-20, what did I learn from this attitude challenge? Simply this — I was not Superman, and I did not know it all. I may have had life experiences before, but the blind world was one to which I needed to adapt safely. I needed to be aware of my surroundings, pay attention to details, both of which were important for my safety. No one cared if I made wallets, rugs, stools, lamps, cooked, or any number of other things I could do. What mattered was that I learn to do many things and do them with care.

I still get impatient with many things in my life, but the lessons I learned in the rehab classes have stayed with me to this day. I'm usually very aware and very careful in my daily activities. In the Army I ran a lot; I don't run anymore. I do walk faster than most blind people, but it is because I use a dog now and not a cane. That is another story for later.

After a few weeks of training, I was allowed to venture out at night with the other guys. That usually turned into an adventure of some sort. The Lemon Drop Inn was a bar with country music, and it was across a main street which ran next to the main hospital. By now, we all knew how to get off the hospital grounds. So, beer and girls, "look out — here we come!"

Four of us went to the club one night for burgers and beer. It was great. Then the music started. Well, little did we know that the place had more women than men, and the ladies wanted to dance. Being bold, four of the women came over. Each of the women snagged one of us, told us to leave our canes, and pulled us to the dance floor for some slow dancing. Well, I knew how to slow dance. I had been well-schooled by Miss Flint in the steps for ballroom dancing but now without the handkerchief. My partner was, how should I say this, large plus. She had a beehive hairdo that tickled my nose, huge boobs that she gladly pressed into my ribs, and she was wide at the beam, so much so that I didn't think my hands would touch if I tried to hug her. Come on song, end.

The song did end but another started up, again slow, and my large and friendly partner just kept on holding me close and dancing. She wanted to dance. Finally after three songs, I told her I had to use the men's room. She reluctantly let me go by showing me to the room. I told her I needed my cane. She got it for me, and off we went.

The other guys had the same idea after being shanghaied by the women. We decided to go to our table and pay our bill. If they asked, we would tell them that the rehab had a curfew, and we needed to get back. We got out of there in a hurry and managed to eventually find our way back to our rooms, albeit later than if we were sober. We found other bars after that for nightly outings.

Social life was practically none, but there was a weekly social night at the facility. Volunteers would come, bring snacks and soft drinks for the guys, and music would play on the radio. I met several nice people at these socials. Pat Knoblauch was a volunteer whom I got to know reasonably well. She would visit me on weekends, and we would walk the hospital grounds. I always felt independent and did not necessarily want to hold Pat's arm. I started wandering in the grass until I ran smack into a low-hanging tree branch that hit my face and put me flat on my back. Pat came over to me and innocently inquired, "Well Hotshot, do you still want to do this walk by yourself?" I regained my feet, swallowed my injured pride and took her arm.

On occasion, I would visit her and her two kids at their nearby home. We would have dinner, talk about lots of things, go on outings in Chicago, and we stayed in touch for years after I left the program. Ten years later, her daughter, seven when I knew her in Chicago, visited me in San Diego when she moved to California.

My training was winding down. For recreation, I would work out in the gym now and then, but mostly I would read books in my spare time. I would get frustrated at times when wondering about what to do with my life. I was given some aptitude tests, and the results pointed to furthering my education, perhaps in law. I had not thought about it, but I had to do something. In the fall of 1969, I applied to the law schools at my alma mater, University of Richmond, William & Mary College, and Denver University.

I knew I was eligible for substantial VA benefits for rehab and that also meant my school costs would be covered by the government. I could live on my disability check. I had the choice of retired pay as a first lieutenant or VA pay based on disability. It was a no-brainer, as the VA benefit was about 3 times as much because of my disability.

I used to hit golf balls into a net on weekends when the weather was nice. I knew a bit about golf from my sighted days, but there were a lot of hard whiffs and frustration when trying to hit a ball I could not see. I figure that I was compensating for starting to be angry about being blind.

Every vet in the program got to know Dr. Beatriz Klich. She was a psychologist who was concerned about our mental health and our ability to cope after losing our sight. I remember telling her during our first meeting that I was just fine. I was happy, adjusted, enjoying the program, and ready to move on. She didn't buy it. We had several sessions, but she could not get me to open up about my feelings. My stubborn Polish heritage was alive and well.

When it came time to finally leave, I stopped in to say goodbye to her. She looked at me and said, in her slightly Brazilian accented voice, "David, you are one tough nut to crack."

It would be many years later before I realized that I suffered from what came to be known as Post Traumatic Stress Disorder. Dr. Klich no doubt knew it was going to happen when she counseled me at Hines. I was too stubborn to realize that a crash and burn scenario was looming in my future. Had I not been so hard-headed, I might have saved myself several years of drift and depression.

Some thirty years later, I saw her at a convention of the Blinded Veterans Association, and we spoke to each other. She asked if I was still a tough nut. I smiled at her and said, "You remembered that, and so do I. I think I've mellowed just a little over time."

My training with Woody was nearly at an end, too. I did well in the program, so well, that I was ready to go out into the world after 12 weeks, not 16 or more. The final week consisted of ordering a variety of equipment the VA was giving me. I got a large reel-to-reel tape recorder, talking time pieces, including a self-winding watch with a pop up crystal which I still have to this day and which still works, a braille machine, a slate and stylus for writing braille by hand and a new cane. I would be going to my parents to await the results of my law school applications. Meanwhile, the final test of my mobility skills with Woody was waiting for me.

Drop offs was the term given to the mobility finale. There were ten final sessions, two a day. Woody would come to my room and just say, "David, go to the Woolworth's store on Main Street," and he would just walk away. So, cane in hand, off I would go. I left the rehab wing and headed toward the hospital and the street crossing area on the way to the store. I knew where it was, and how to get there safely. I was very confident with my cane skills. It took about thirty minutes, and Woody was waiting for me when I arrived. Another test involved Woody dropping me off on the sidewalk of an overpass to a busy, noisy freeway and telling me to meet him at the library. The first task was to figure out if you were on the right or wrong side of the overpass. If wrong, I had to recall how to safely get to the other side. My sense of direction is good, but better if the sun is out, and I know what time of day it is. I did this task correctly, too. There were eight more drop offs. Some were easy and took no time. Find the bakery, and I would be dropped in front of the store next to it. I simply followed my nose. I would get into the car with Woody, and he would drive and drive. He would turn into a driveway and seemingly just make turns. He would be in a lot and drive in circles just to confuse me. Then he would tell me to get out and go somewhere. I recall walking about six blocks in one direction listening to traffic and other noises, like a clock striking the hour, sensing the sun, hearing a train whistle, or a bus stopping before finally figuring out where I was and where I needed to go.

The final test was the longest. Woody and I were dropped on Lake Street, and he told me where we were. He simply said, "Go to your room."

So, I began the hour long walk from Lake Street to the hospital. This involved using everything I learned during training. There were uneven sidewalks, overhanging trees which canes do not identify, street crossings with and without traffic signals, yield intersections where traffic does not always yield, and parking meters to avoid. They can hurt if you walk off line and miss one with your cane. I was painfully reminded of that more than once early in training. I also learned that getting mad at the meter and hitting it just meant that both your shoulder and hand now hurt. I crossed freeway overpasses with noise from traffic so loud that staying oriented was a challenge. I found that wind and rain distorted sound. They caused the greatest challenge to my mobility. A blind person needs to hear sound differentiations for direction. I rode the L train into Chicago, negotiated the train stations, found my way to a major hotel, and returned by bus all alone. That challenge built up my self-confidence.

I made it back to the hospital in 50 minutes, a record and with no mishaps. Woody shook my hand and told me I was one of his best students ever. I knew I was confident and very good with the cane.

However, as part of blindness training, we had a visit from Bob Whitstock of The Seeing Eye Guide Dog Program. I attended his talk and by his side was Nesta, his German Shepherd guide dog. I never forgot that meeting. I saw the ease of movement Bob had with his dog. I started thinking about a dog. I contacted The Seeing Eye and applied. I was accepted for the last class of 1969 in December to get a dog at Morristown, New Jersey.

The staff of the VA, especially Woody and John Malamazian, understood the draw of a dog. They both told me I was an excellent cane user, but even if I used a dog, there would be times when I would need those cane skills. They were correct, of course.

I went home for a few days to repack for a three week stay in New Jersey to get my first dog, Jon. He was a German Shepherd and would be the first of 6 wonderful companions who, to this day, have guided me, loved me, needed me as much as I needed them, and were and are a calming influence in my life.

I have never forgotten the lessons learned during my VA rehab. Those skills have been a part of my life for the last 49 years. The VA is currently under scrutiny for its lack of care to veterans, but I am one veteran who benefited greatly from VA programs and have only high praise for their programs and care.

I trained with my first Seeing Eye dog, Jon. After four weeks of training, I went home to Gloversville with Jon in time for Christmas. What a wonderful present I had that year. And, the two years of allergy shots I took weekly during my first two years of college had paid off. I did not have a dog allergy anymore. I still can't be around cats though. Jon was a welcome addition to me and my family at Christmas 1969. Everyone was home for the holiday, and I recall wrestling on the floor with Tim. Jon got anxious at this rough-housing and grabbed onto Tim's leg and started to pull him away from me.

Rich and Steve were cracking up, and Tim was yelling. Mom came to see what the fuss and noise was and saw Tim's leg in Jon's mouth. She covered her face, began to cry and went into the kitchen. Steve asked her if she was upset, and she said that she wasn't. She was glad to know that a big German Shepherd was going to look out for David.

I had seen Mom cry months earlier when home on leave from Walter Reed. I asked why she was crying, and she simply said, "Oh, Honey, you are just so young to have had this happen to you. It makes me very sad." I tried to ease her concerns but probably did not do a very good job of it. She became more comfortable as I completed rehab, got a dog, lived with a friend and got into law school.

It was the dead of winter at home, but Jon and I ventured out most days to walk. Naturally, I knew Gloversville's streets, so getting lost was not my concern. Eventually I got bored staying home, so I decided to visit my friends back in Richmond. Richard Sinclair finished his Vietnam service and returned to finish his BA degree after a short break from school. I saw him and went to some classes with him. Jon was by my side. I then learned what a chick magnet my dog was. Meeting girls was a bit easier with a friendly dog. I kept telling anyone who wanted him that we were a package deal. Apparently, that line got old quickly.

I saw several of my younger fraternity brothers and stayed with some for a few days. While there, I received notice at home that I was accepted for law school at Denver University. I was disappointed that the University of Richmond did not accept my application. The rejection stung especially harshly when the law school dean wrote in the letter that he did not feel blind people should be in the legal field as the work would be far too difficult. I was very angry with his response. Years later, when I graduated from law school, I copied my degree and sent it to him with a copy of his rejection letter. Unfortunately, he had passed away, but his widow sent me a gracious letter congratulating me for my success.

6

Law School

My good friend and fraternity brother, Dick Peterson, lived and worked in Denver. He was single and said we could share an apartment if I wanted. I did, and I returned home to pack and make a final move from Gloversville. In the spring of 1970, I flew to Denver and moved in with Dick. Jon was the hit of the apartment building, and I had six months before starting law school. During that time, I learned the layout of my Denver neighborhood. I also learned the route to walk to the school which, in those days, was in the downtown area of Denver and not at the Denver University campus.

Jon and I had many adventures. I was in a new part of the country and with that came new kinds of food. I remember taking a date out for Mexican food one evening. I had never had it before that night. I sat down at the table and put my napkin in my lap noting that it was quite warm. I told my friend that the napkin seemed very warm. She said, "That is because it is your tortilla, and now you have flour on your pants." I did the only thing left to do and started to munch on my "napkin." Over the years and at many conventions with other blind individuals, we would always laugh about how only blind people eat parsley, orange rinds, lemon wedges, and other assorted garnishes.

I would spend time at the pool at our building getting to know other tenants. Our building shared a pool with another building, and I met Gail Ireland one day. He was a lawyer and the former Attorney-General of Colorado. He and I spoke often of the law, and he took a keen interest in my schooling over the next three years. I also met a lady there who, just prior to starting school, became my wife. We were married back near Gloversville, as my parents put on the wedding. Obviously, this was a very fast romance and the odds of success were quite low. There is more to a relationship than sex and a pretty face. I'm sure that there was some apprehension on my part that no woman would want me in her life with my injury. I was also reasonably well off financially on a monthly basis, so maybe she saw some stability and that could overcome other issues. There was strain in our marriage and suffice it to say, we should never have married. I was a law student and very involved with school. I did not have much time for her, and it became apparent that a split was coming. We lasted about a year and then she returned to her home state. She and I had moved into another building, so when she left, I simply stayed. I was on VA benefits for both disability and schooling, so I could afford to stay. We had no children, so the break up was fairly clean.

Law school started in September. I was one of five blind students to enroll in the experiment Denver University was offering. None of us were required to take the law school entrance exam. I took the required classes and used a tape recorder in all classes.

Many of my books were on reel to reel tapes, but those that were not were read to me either by other students in law school, or undergrads who I hired and paid hourly with VA funds. One law student who has been a lifelong friend was Dawson Joyner. We took several courses together, and he got paid to read the text to me as he read the material for himself.

I felt like I went to law school twice. I recorded my daily lectures, and each evening, I listened to them again and spoke into a second recorder outlining the things I thought were important. This went on for three years with every class. I would then study the condensed notes and make up braille notes to help me remember when exam time came. I studied hard and passed my courses. I attended summer school each summer and thus was able to graduate in March of 1973. I took the Colorado bar exam in February of that year and passed it. I was proud. Jon was now a legal beagle of sorts.

My personal life was pretty much on hold during law school. I did not date much, but stayed friends with Dick Peterson and Dawson

Joyner, along with one or two other law school buddies. Dean Phillips was a law student and good friend to have if you wanted to shoot the breeze about the Army. He was a Vietnam vet who was more involved with veterans' affairs than law school affairs, and he eventually went to work for the VA in Washington, DC. He passed away from cancer caused by Agent Orange many years later.

I applied for a job with the federal government with the Equal Employment Opportunity Commission. I was offered the job as an attorney. Unfortunately, I did not find the work interesting and stayed only three months. In hindsight, I'm not sure I had really come to terms with my blindness. I felt a bit lost in the greater scheme of things.

Several years had gone by since my injury. I still wore dark glasses and needed to have my eyes evaluated. It became clear that the damage was extensive and permanent. My eyes were not visually appealing. The VA ophthalmologists discussed my options, and I opted to have them enucleated. The surgery took place, and the remainder of my natural eyes were extracted. My eye muscles were not damaged, so they were stitched into a ball of material which took the shape of my eye socket. I could now be fitted for prosthetic eyes. Soon, I would meet with an ocularist in the VA system who would make me my first pair of plastic eyes. I had my first pair made blue, although my birth eyes were brown with one a bit greener. Now they were dark blue. Over the next 43 years, I would have several sets made with each set being a lighter blue than the previous ones.

I did not need dark glasses. Even today, most people who meet me do not know my eyes are not real. I have good muscle control, and I am able to track conversation and movement of others enough that they think I can see.

Now I was sporting new eyes, had a great dog, lived alone and did not have a job. I also gave up smoking as I finished law school. That was a very good thing.

So, although tobacco was now gone, alcohol was not. Now began some years of struggle for me. The focused life of rehab and law school were over, and I was now forced to face each day without any real purpose. I needed to come to grips with my blindness. Little did I know that it would take the next four years of my life to get some positive direction.

7

The Struggle

It was the summer of 1973. I was living at my apartment in a Denver highrise. I was out of school, living with my guide dog Jon, having no reason to get up other than to take the dog outside, and facing another day of wondering what to do. I knew my parents were worried about me following my disclosure that I left the EEOC job. My mother suggested that my brother Tim come for a visit. He was 14 now, and a week with me might be good for both of us. I agreed, and he flew out to Denver.

Tim and I talked about who knows what, but we had a good time. We went out to dinner a time or two with Dawson and maybe Dick Peterson. Tim got to meet many of the people I knew in the apartment building as we hung out by the pool most days. I was working on a killer tan while just being a bum.

Tim would take Jon out for me and take him on short walks. We would watch television, too. Before he left to go home, I hosted a small party for friends in the building. Many came, and Tim proudly played bartender. Little did I know that he sampled a few of the drinks as he worked. It was later that night that I heard him puking and no doubt learning one of life's lessons. Fortunately, he had a day to recover before flying home. We made a solemn promise to each other that Mom and Dad would never learn of his indiscretion and my child neglect.

I read a lot of books during this low period of my life. I didn't really look for work. I would get books from the Library of Congress on either records or tape and sit for hours reading. It was an escape.

I probably read a book or two a week. I used to record in braille the title of every book I read, but I stopped recording the titles thirty years or more ago when I had over 1500 titles. I threw the list away.

The days went by and the afternoons brought happy hour daily. More often than not, I would drink beer. Often many cans a day would lead me to an early night in the sack. Early nights mean early wakeups. I was awake before most of Denver. I would start reading in the wee hours and continue until the sun was up and warm enough to go to the pool and crash. As summer ended and the pool was not an option, I would take naps to escape the boredom. I would awake and have a beer. I would eat well, but I could see that I had no direction. I would talk with friends, and they would encourage me, but there wasn't much they could do to help me find my way.

My law school friend Dawson lived in the same building, and we would go out for a huge Mexican dinner at a local favorite spot and have drinks with dinner. We would go to the grocery store, get two carts and load up on everything from dog food to whatever I needed. We would spend a lot of money on my food haul, but it would be another month before we did it again. He would always help me unload and stock the cabinets. I always knew we drank too much when the soup cans ended up on the canned dog food shelf. I thought Jon's food was a bit watery at times and smelled surprisingly good.

It was football season again, and I was a big Denver Broncos fan. I would go to Bronco rally lunches with a friend in the building. We would often watch the game on Sunday if he didn't go to the game.

I had many good friends in my apartment building. They knew of my war injury and subsequent completion of law school. They admired me for that, but I don't think they admired the way I was wasting my life.

This aimless wandering without purpose went on for the better part of two years. During that time, I began to realize that I was not handling being blind very well. I always felt I was in control of any situation. I was tired of being sad, lonely and depressed. I knew that I could either get out of this rut or wallow in self-pity until something bad happened. I knew I was drinking too much, and my days and nights got flipped around. Something had to give. Resilience from this low point was slow in developing. I did not want my mood to be the reason friends avoided me.

I cannot tell you when the light clicked on for me. I knew I wanted more out of life. I began to think that Denver was not the answer for me. I was not sure where I wanted to go, but the thought of moving from Denver began to take shape. Then, I got the call from my brother Rich telling me that Dad was dead from a tragic accident. He fell from a ladder while working. I went home for the funeral, and I got very emotional during the service. I realized that while Dad and I were close, we did not express our emotions to one another often. I wished I had told him how much I loved him. Mom hugged me and told me that Dad was very proud of me.

Naturally, Mom was devastated and leaned on her boys for emotional support. I was able to provide some financial help to her, as the window washing business did not provide any retirement. Tim was just 15 and still in high school. To Mom's credit, she never suggested I move home, even though she knew I was struggling in Denver. We buried Dad, and I helped get Mom organized before returning to Denver. She retired from her nursing job a few years later and remarried. Her second husband was very different from Dad, but he was nice to Mom, especially after she discovered she had cancer. She lost that battle at the age of 65, nine years after Dad's accidental death.

Upon my return to Denver following Dad's death, I knew I had to get out of my rut and find my purpose in life. I thought Hawaii might be a fun place to live and find work. I inquired and learned there was a six month quarantine for dogs before they could be allowed to roam freely on the islands. That rule ended any thought of Hawaii. I would not put Jon in a kennel for six months.

I mentally retraced my steps back east from Hawaii and decided to move to San Diego. It had great weather, was not too big, and it was home to the Navy where my retired military status would give me access to the bases. I was hopeful that I could get a new start there. Now, I needed to get organized to move. I started drinking less, and I began to look forward to a new beginning.

In January of 1976, I went out in a blizzard one night and took a cab to a bar. Hardly anyone was there, but two guys from Georgia were there, and we talked. They were headed to a different bar and asked if I wanted to go. I did, and I went with them.

There, I met two women they knew, and one was named Janice Bonial. I eventually asked her out, and she said yes. Our first date was dinner at my place with steak, baked potatoes and wine. It was only later that Janice told me that she changed her clothes three times before deciding what to wear. We laughed about it, because she was so concerned about how she looked for truly a blind date. I must have made a good impression because I learned much later that she told her girlfriend that she met the guy she was going to marry.

Janice and I had a good time together and saw each other often. It was tough for me as I was really starting to like her, and I knew I was going to leave Denver soon. When I told her, she was supportive and offered to go with me to help me find an apartment and get settled. She did, and I settled in Pacific Beach near the ocean. Janice went back to her job in Denver, and we corresponded by cassette tape.

I got involved with a congressional campaign during that summer, and it kept me busy while I sought a paying job. A job was not forthcoming for a while, but at least San Diego was warm and the people were friendly. I met some great folks at World Famous, a restaurant on the beach at the boardwalk. It was about three short blocks from my apartment. I went there on most nights for dinner and drinks and ran a tab which I paid monthly. The political candidate lost the November election, so nothing would come of that volunteer effort.

Janice and I had become closer by sharing thoughts and feelings on tape and making occasional phone calls. I asked her if she would consider moving to San Diego to live with me. She agreed, and she arrived in January 1977. We moved three times before finally settling in our first home.

Living together was a new experience for both of us, as we had lived alone in the recent past. I had certain obvious rules in my living situation which came naturally. Doors were not left ajar, pathways were always clear of objects, items were placed in a location for a simple reason — so I could easily find them again. It was a learning experience for Janice, too. She had to remember that I could not see, so daily activity might present a dangerous situation if she was not careful. The best example is leaving a door partially open so that the hallway was not completely free of the obstruction. I had run into many open doors and had bruises to show for it.

There were minor frustrations at times, such as when pill bottles got switched from the position I had left them in, or toothpaste and medical cream got their positions switched. Eventually we compromised on the big things, and I learned to remain calm when the little things were not exactly the way I would have preferred.

Janice found work in the computer field in the northern part of San Diego so we looked for another place to live. We went house hunting and found a home in a small subdivision named Cardiff by the Sea. We bought that house for about $70,000. It had four bedrooms and a pool.

Earlier that year, I made a contact in the San Diego office of the VA, and I was offered a job by Dan Emer, the Chief of the benefits counselors and a service rep of the VA who worked in Vietnam. He had worked in other VA facilities and knew of a blinded World War II vet named Bill Hasse. Bill was coming to work in San Diego also. Dan introduced me to Bill, and he showed me the ropes as I trained to be a benefits counselor with the VA. Bill taught me much about the VA. He had forgotten more about the VA than I would ever know. We became very close friends, and he relied on Janice for many things during his time here before he got married. He was also a positive role model for me, as he had learned to handle blindness and be productive, too. He was my inspiration to strive for success.

So, I had a job, bought a house, and in March 1978, Janice and I were married. Bill was a witness, as was a couple who also worked at the VA. It appeared that my self-pity days and aimless wandering were over now. I did not know that there were still some challenges ahead. Janice and I entertained neighbors, had pool parties, poker nights, and experienced the struggles of newlyweds.

I was getting restless at the VA and felt like I needed a new challenge. I wanted to take the California bar exam and try to get a law license. So, I left the VA in 1981 and studied for the exam. Janice and I were together but distant emotionally. She had a job, and I did not. She loved me with heart and soul, but I had difficulty responding and reciprocating. My emotional blindness led to our eventual separation and divorce. Later, after we reunited, we discovered that we were often thinking about each other while we were apart.

8

Looking Forward

Janice and I set up our household in Cardiff in 1978. I had been working for nearly a year as a veteran's counselor for the San Diego VA by then. Cardiff by the Sea was a fairly long drive to work, but there were a few coworkers who also lived in the north county area. I soon hooked up with one or more of them for rides to and from work in exchange for help with gasoline.

I loved the pool at our house and tried to keep up with my fitness routine using a total gym machine, weights in the garage, and swimming in the pool. For a while, I was able to swim a mile when I had the time to do it.

Jon seemed happy to walk in our neighborhood. He was getting on in years, and I could tell that he was having difficulty walking at times. Eventually, as is the case with many large dogs, he developed degenerative disk issues and started to drag a hind leg. The hardest decision I had to make was to put him down and stop his suffering.

My coping with blindness was beginning to manifest itself in negative ways. I was becoming remote with Janice, and we often felt strain in our marriage. I was not a big believer in counseling, but I did talk with professionals on occasion and once relived the day of my injury. It was the first time I really talked with anyone about it. I felt like a weight was lifted from my shoulders. I could hear Dr. Klich saying, "I was a tough nut to crack."

I was becoming restless with my job. While I was performing my work well and helping veterans, I started to feel pigeonholed. I thought I could do more than just counsel vets for a career. I started to think about taking the California Bar exam and trying to be a lawyer.

My friend Bill Hasse was also a lawyer, but he was from an earlier era when acceptance and assistance for the blind were rare. He had a family to care for, and the VA job opportunity satisfied his immediate needs. He encouraged me to take the exam and make a go of lawyering.

In the fall of 1980, I left the VA and began the refresher course for the February 1981 bar exam. I studied very hard and took the exam with the help of a sighted co-worker of Janice's. He and I were sequestered in a local motel room with a proctor in the same room. She had the exam, and I was given time and a half to answer the essays and multiple choice questions over the three days of the exam. The proctor sat on the bed in the room and read a magazine all day, each day. My reader would read the questions, and I would choose the multiple choice answer, and dictate essay answers which he would write in blue booklets. I stayed in that room for two nights.

After the exam, while waiting for results, I returned to the The Seeing Eye to obtain my second dog. He was also a German Shepherd but with the traditional black and tan coat. He was huge, weighing in at 79 pounds when I got him. He was a beautiful dog, but he had issues with loud noises, so trying to keep him calm in a night club was a chore.

I waited for three months for the exam results. In the meantime, Janice and I decided to separate. She moved out and into an apartment in Carlsbad. We decided to get a divorce. In May, I got the bar exam results, and I did not pass. I was a half point shy of passing. I appealed the decision, but it did not change. Now I was upset, alone, and in a big house with my new dog OJ. I was sad and depressed through that summer, but I was determined to try again to pass the exam. I would take it in early 1982.

I had heard of the national veteran's organization of blinded vets known as the BVA. I decided to attend their convention in 1980 in Los Angeles. I attended and met many Vietnam vets along with older blinded vets. I thought the comradery and commonality of disability and interest would be good for me. I spoke on the convention floor and made my name known.

The BVA was governed by a board of directors with regional responsibility. I decided I would run for the district covering California. I wrote an introductory letter about myself and my qualifications and mailed it to the entire district. I won the election, unseating a long time dedicated person who had held most of the national offices and the district seat for years. He congratulated me, and we became friends in the ensuing years. I held the regional seat for many three-year terms. Then, I ran for and was elected to the positions of National Secretary, Vice-President, and President. My greatest honor came when I represented the BVA during Congressional testimony before the House and Senate Veterans Affairs Committees. I had the privilege of attending the Inauguration of President Bush in 1989 and meeting the President, Mrs. Bush, Vice-President Quail and his wife at the Inaugural Ball.

I had reorganized the San Diego chapter of the BVA and brought local blinded veterans together to help establish a presence in San Diego. I was the local President for many years and then the Treasurer. The chapter is still active in the area, although I am no longer an active participant.

Through the national BVA, I was introduced to the director of the Federal Action Agency. He was developing a program known as the Vietnam Veterans Leadership Program, and there would be an office in San Diego. He offered me the position of Executive Director. I was to find an office, develop an outreach effort with business leaders to advise and mentor Vietnam vets in their efforts to get back into society and find training and jobs. The thrust of the program was to help change the negative image of Vietnam veterans that had developed near the end of the war and beyond.

I studied for and again took the bar exam in February 1982, and then hired an office assistant to help me organize the VVLP. Jan Dodge was her name, and she was involved with the Vietnam POW-MIA effort. Her Navy pilot husband had been shot down during the war. He was a known prisoner, but he did not return when the POWs were released. Her interest in the program and assistance to me was invaluable.

In May of 1982, I learned that I had passed the bar exam this time. I was very relieved. I had been making significant local contacts for the VVLP and now had a law license also in my quiver.

VVLP did many good things in San Diego to raise positive awareness of veteran contributions to society. We highlighted the many skills and experiences that a veteran could bring to a job. We worked closely with Jack Lyon and his Vietnam Veterans of San Diego organization. They were initially wary of VVLP, but we eventually discovered that we wanted the same thing, to help veterans. We worked together to help open a rehab home and that small step forward eventually grew into a substantial, multi-purpose rehabilitation, job training, psychological treatment, drug and alcohol counseling effort in the San Diego area funded with donations and grant money in the millions of dollars. VVSD and Veterans Village is a nationwide model of what a community can do for its veterans.

While in VVLP, one of our advisors was a retired Brigadier Marine General named Edward Meyer. He and I worked closely and became friends. One day I told him that I was going to leave the VVLP program. I told him that I had passed the bar exam and did not want to be a professional veteran. He understood and stayed close to me throughout my future career. He introduced me to those who would profoundly affect the future course of my legal career. He was a close friend until his death in 2004. His wife Ann remained close friends with Janice and me for twelve more years until she also passed away.

I turned over the operation of the VVLP to a new director, and Jan Dodge also decided to move on to other interests. Now it was time to find a new job.

I interviewed with some law firms and the local energy company. Many of the business contacts I made with VVLP gave me leads. I had advisors on the board who were attorneys also, and they encouraged me.

Tom Christisen and Fred Martin offered to let me office with their firm for a share of expenses. They would try to funnel me some work, too.

So, I borrowed $50,000 from the Small Business Administration and went into private practice. I furnished my office, a bit too nicely as it turned out. I did not need such expensive furnishings. I hired a secretary and research person. I helped the firm with some of their tedious work, and they paid me for my time. I went to many seminars to become known in the legal community. I joined a breakfast club of professionals to help get business. From the breakfast group, I met Steve Kuhn, a young accountant. We became friends and to this day he handles my tax work.

I joined a group of young Republicans to further help spread my name in the community. I also participated in a mock political campaign retreat weekend which propelled me into taking a more active interest in politics.

The effort to succeed in my law practice was good, but the result was not. I had just a few clients with no prospects for more and no more money. I had to leave the sole practitioner business and again try to find a job.

During this period, Janice and I had been divorced. I sold the Cardiff house and moved into an apartment in San Diego within walking distance of the law office. I dated different women during this time, but I kept thinking of Janice.

One night shortly before leaving the law office practice, I had dinner with Tom and told him that I had been thinking of Janice and missed her. He said that if I really missed her and cared about her, then I should swallow my pride and try to contact her. I gave that some thought and made a tape to her expressing myself and my feelings about having made a mistake by calling it quits with her. I didn't know where she was, but an acquaintance had her address. I sent the tape to her. It got lost in the mail, and I heard that she did not receive it, so I sent another one which she did receive.

Soon after receiving the tape, Janice contacted me, and we set up a meeting on neutral ground. I took a cab to Old Town, a part of San Diego, and met her. We talked about the tape, hurt feelings, feelings for and about each other, and whether we should try again. We decided to see each other and see how it went. Janice knew that I had recently lost my Mother to cancer.

She had known my mother, and they had gotten along well.

We dated and things were going well with us. I still did not have a job, but I had income from the VA. We decided that we should try to make the relationship work. She had a condo in northern San Diego, and I had some money from the sale of the Cardiff home. We decided to put the money together and find a place to start fresh. We chose Coronado as a place to start. It was over the Coronado Bridge and was known as the island, although the strand connected it to Imperial Beach to the south. We found a nice condo, and we were able to put down enough of a payment to qualify for a loan to purchase it. It was the spring of 1985, and we remarried in May. Ed Meyer arranged for us to have a reception at the Navy Amphib base in Coronado after our wedding at St. David's Episcopal Church in San Diego. Reverend William Mehedy was a Vietnam vet I had met through VVSD, and he performed the ceremony. Janice's Mom and brother came to the wedding, as did my brothers Rich and Tim. Many of my veteran friends, some attorneys, acquaintances and my cousin Paula attended. Paula was like a sister to me and for many years she lived in San Diego. She recently passed away, but I am blessed to have her daughter Kristin living here now. I was finally happy and looking forward to making my life purposeful.

9

A Career

Janice, OJ and I settled into life in Coronado following our remarriage. We had a nice three bedroom condo within walking distance of the beach and business district of Coronado. The North Island Naval Air Station was also close and available to us.

We became friends with our neighbors in the five unit condo complex, and we are still very close to Karen and Joe Maggio. I actively sought work and began to go to the courthouse in San Diego to observe court activity.

1985 came to a close and a new member of the family joined us at Christmas. No, it was not a baby. Janice and I decided to not have children. I was nearly 40 and she nearly 39 when we remarried. Our new addition was Boo. She was an African Grey parrot, and she was born that spring. I had always wanted a parrot. It was not long before she was talking, and we learned to be careful about what we said because she would mimic us perfectly. We would add two more parrots to the household before we stopped gathering feathered friends. They require significant care and attention. Those duties primarily fell to Janice. Their daily feeding and cage cleaning became a ritual for her. Traveling on vacation always presents a challenge for us as finding someone for bird care is not easy. They have been fun, funny, a source of noise to remind us we are not alone, and a joyful enrichment to our lives.

I had followed job opening announcements with the city of San Diego's attorney office and the county's District Attorney's office. I applied to both and interviewed for a job with both. I recall being very nervous as I met with three prosecutors from the DA's office. They asked me some general questions about my life, posed some legal questions for a response, and the interview ended. I received a second interview from the DA with two other senior deputies and that meeting was more relaxed. They wanted to know what it would take to help make me successful as a prosecutor. I told them I had a reading machine that read printed material, but a sighted assistant would also be necessary. They inquired as to whether I could pay for that help. I indicated that I would take it out of my pay if necessary. A week later, they offered me the job starting at a $25,000 salary. They would allow me to hire a paralegal, and the DA would pay for that person. I have to thank Patrick Russell, a DA investigator whom I knew through work with veterans groups, for vouching for me when the District Attorney inquired about me before making his final decision to hire me. I was thrilled, and so was Janice. I started my legal career in March 1986 as a Deputy District Attorney assigned to prosecute criminal cases.

I worked in the Welfare Fraud Section and received great support from its lead prosecutor, Ralph Fear. I learned the ins and outs of prosecuting welfare fraud and eventually hired Patricia Brammer as my paralegal. Pat and I worked well as a team for over ten years until a rare health issue forced her to retire.

We issued cases, concluded plea bargains for guilty pleas, occasionally presented preliminary hearings to judges showing evidence of crime which supported a defendant's guilt, and had a great time doing it. After one year in welfare fraud, Pat and I were transferred to the South Bay branch office in Chula Vista. I rode the bus to and from work when in downtown San Diego, and that continued for the hour long bus ride to Chula Vista. Soon however, I started riding to work with another prosecutor who also lived in Coronado. George Bennet and I became good friends on those rides, and often we would just go out for dinner and shoot the breeze. Later, we would play golf together and recall those old days.

During my first year in the office, I received wonderful support from the other attorneys and staff in the office. They were naturally curious as to how I was going to approach the work assignments, but my work ethic was instilled in me long before I was blinded. I was at work early, stayed late, took work home and spent more hours on cases in the evenings and on weekends. I didn't do more than other attorneys, but I knew that my success depended on my preparation. As the years went by, I became more confident of my ability to do the job without burning myself out with extra time on cases. My advancement through the office and promotions settled the question of whether or not I could be an effective prosecutor.

South Bay was the true learning lab for being a trial attorney. As a new prosecutor with little court experience, I was given experience in many aspects of prosecution. I issued misdemeanor cases, wrote motions, settled cases, tried misdemeanor cases before a jury, argued sentencing issues, graduated to issuing felonies, and presented preliminary hearings to the court. I spent four years with Pat Brammer in Chula Vista becoming one of the senior lawyers in that office. The highlight of my years there came when I was assigned to prosecute cases that arose from crimes committed in the nearby state prison facility. Yes, criminals do commit crimes against other criminals.

Most of the prison cases resulted in guilty pleas, and the inmates received consecutive prison sentences which tacked on more time to their original term of years. Sometimes, they required a trial. Those were especially interesting as a jury would hear testimony from one convicted defendant who was a witness now testifying against another convicted inmate. Most of those cases resulted in guilty verdicts, but one did not, and it was because the jury felt the witness inmate was a liar and more frightening than the defendant. Win some, lose some!

While investigating prison cases, I would often have to go to the prison to interview witnesses. It was always dicey when Pat and I, along with OJ, my German Shepherd guide dog, would stroll into the inmate yard accompanied by several armed guards. We would get the evil-eye look as we walked, but most inmates did not want more trouble and OJ was intimidating. I later learned from guards that the inmates did not believe I was a DA nor that I was blind. They thought OJ was a drug dog.

It was in Chula Vista that I was first supervised by Ed Checkert. He gave me pointers on negotiating pleas. I held the job of settling cases prior to my transfer back into San Diego. Eight years later, Ed would be one of my last supervisors in the office, but we had become friends. Now, thirty years later, we still talk with each other weekly and socialize occasionally.

While in Chula Vista, I became friends with Tom Basinski, a District Attorney Investigator. We would get together for beers now and then, and soon, Ed Checkert and his wife, Tom and his wife, and Janice and I would do couples nights out two or three times a year. Often, we rotated dinners at each other's homes, and always had an Octoberfest meal with German and Polish food. Tom and I formed the Polish Brotherhood and became confidants about many topics over the years. He and I would golf together and meet on Sunday mornings at the golf range to hit buckets of balls and just shoot the breeze as friends do. He recently passed away from cancer. I miss our times together greatly.

The Chula Vista experience afforded me the opportunity to move to the San Diego Superior Court division of the office. Here, Pat and I shared a large office to work our cases. This was the big show for prosecutors unless assigned to one of many specialized divisions. The Super court division, as we were known, handled everything from robbery, to murder and most every other felony in between. Theft, violence, drugs, arson, you name it, we prosecuted it.

There were special units to handle major narcotics, child abuse, career criminal cases, sexual assaults, gangs, major fraud, and other special cases. Those that carried political or other significant community interests and had the potential to be sensitive or impact the political winds of the office were assigned to more experienced attorneys in these units.

Pat and I were content to delve into the run of the mill felony matters that came our way. My first felony trial was a robbery case defended by a very experienced defense attorney. I knew the trial procedures, how to present my case, how to argue evidence to a jury, and how to argue for a proper sentence if the jury found a defendant guilty. They did, and I won my first felony trial.

I was in my element. As a blind attorney, research would always involve the help of someone else. Technological advances today allow for access to almost all research with computers adapted for a blind user using a speech program. There are also sophisticated scanners that convert text to speech. A technically competent blind person today can do most research and writing unassisted. As a trial attorney, I had help preparing the case, but in court, it was all up to me. I knew the questions to ask the witnesses, I listened carefully to their testimony, needed to think on my feet when addressing the court, and marshalled my arguments to the court or jury. I may not have sold vacuum cleaners, china or pots and pans, but over my prosecutorial career, I sold many jurors on the guilt of defendants for crimes they committed. I didn't always win, but it was not for a lack of trying and making the best argument I could with the evidence and witnesses I had.

I recall one case in particular that happened close to home. Not far from my home was a transient hotel where several people could stay cheaply. One night, two tenants got into a fight, and when all was said and done, one of the tenants was dead. The survivor was arrested and charged with murder. I asked my supervisor to let me have the case. He agreed, and Pat and I began to prepare for the preliminary hearing. We put forth sufficient evidence to convince a judge that the crime occurred, and the defendant was likely guilty.

The defendant was claiming that he didn't do it. I had a photo of a mark on the victim's neck which was puzzling. We enhanced the photo and noted a pattern. I employed an expert on mark evidence. He was renowned in San Diego for his expertise. He had looked at the photo and compared the pattern with the sole of the defendant's boot. It was a perfect match. The defendant had kicked the victim in the neck so forcefully that, as the victim's head snapped sideways, the vertebral artery in the victim's neck was torn. The lack of blood to the brain caused the death. The Jury was fascinated by the expert testimony and convicted the defendant of murder. That case presented several evidentiary issues, and it gave me great satisfaction to bring some semblance of justice for the victim and his family.

After prosecuting about forty or so felony trials, including three murder convictions over five years, I transferred with Pat into the preliminary hearing division. I would be one of the senior deputies who would present cases, mentor and train younger deputies, and help negotiate settlements. My final two years in the office were spent settling cases prior to preliminary hearings. Pat and I would prepare notes each day on about twenty cases set for the next day before a settlement judge. I would make an offer to the defense to plead guilty to a charge, and the judge would indicate a sentence. If the defense liked what they heard, there would be a plea and that case was finished. If not, the assigned prosecutor would present witnesses and evidence to a court to move the case closer to a jury trial. When Pat was forced to retire for health reasons, another office paralegal, Larry Stone, came to work with me until I left the office.

At home, Janice and I were doing well. She spent a good amount of time with her mother, who had relocated to Coronado from Florida to be near Janice as she aged.

We added two more members to our flock. Smokey, another African Grey parrot, was a great talker and very smart. I could handle Boo, but Smokey was more inclined to go to Janice. We also rescued a third bird from our local pet shop. It had been left with the shop by its owner for months with no payment for storage and upkeep. We paid the bill and got Buckwheat, a Blue-Fronted Amazon. She was a beautiful bird with a great whistle, but she was not much of a talker. Buckwheat was also a man hater, so I rarely interacted with her if it might result in being bitten. As I write this narrative, Boo is now 33 and still laying an egg now and then. Smokey is about 30 and yakking away daily. We lost Buckwheat due to a health complication in 2016

While I was still working in Chula Vista, Janice and I decided we would like a house. We went walking in Coronado one day and found a home being built on a narrow but long lot in town, about six blocks from our condo. We went in to watch the work being done and talked with the builder. We liked the layout and knew it would be just right for us. We gave the builder a down payment on the house and nego-tiated a few modifications on the building plan and finishing touches. We moved into our new home in early 1989. We kept the condo, and it has been a rental unit for us for the last 29 years. Over the years, we have done a top to bottom remodel to our home, and we are well settled now. Janice switched jobs in 1988. She went to work at North Island for the Navy as a civilian computer systems analyst. She worked there for ten years and left when I changed jobs in 1998. She got more involved with community animal care projects and spent quality time with her mother for five years until her death in 2003 from age related medical complications. Since then, she has devoted her time to the local animal shelter and our church.

I was now in my eleventh year with the District Attorney's office. The elected DA when I was hired was Edwin Miller. He gave me a won-derful break and the opportunity to have a career. I am forever grateful to him for that opportunity. Now, Mr. Miller is out of office, and there is a new DA. He is a former prosecutor in the office hired by Mr. Miller. I did not know Paul Pfingst, but he is the new boss.

I was 52 years old, and I had given thought to being a judge. Becoming a judge is not that easy. One can run for an open seat, but that happens rarely. Another option is to apply to the Governor for an appointment to a vacancy, which occurs when a judge dies in office or retires before his or her six-year term is over. There is a general rule that prosecutors do not run for judge against a sitting judge. I would not have done that anyway, because that is the same as running for political office with all it entails, especially money.

Instead, I applied to then California Governor Pete Wilson. I was a Republican as was he, so that helped immensely. I also knew the Governor slightly from his days as a California Senator. Over the years in the DA's office, I stayed active in the Blinded Veterans Association, remained on their board and held national office, including the Presidency of the BVA. I testified before Congressional veterans committees on veteran issues and met with committee reps and staff in their offices. In this capacity, I met briefly with Senator Wilson.

Paul Pfingst knew I was applying to be a judge, and he brought me to the California DA's association meeting being held in San Diego at which Governor Wilson was speaking. Paul introduced me following the speech. I said hello to the Governor as I stood shaking his hand and holding the leash of Lucky, my third guide dog. I did not say anything about being a judge, but my application was signed and sealed and went into the mail that evening with a cover letter of support from Mr. Pfingst.

The selection process can take some time, and it either happens or it doesn't. I applied in July 1997, and my name was selected for further vetting by the legal community. Forms were sent to judges and attorneys in the county for comment on my qualifications to be a judge. This formal vetting would not have happened had my friend and mentor, Edward Meyer, not introduced me to three judges, two of whom I had worked with before. Dick Murphy presided over many of my trials, and he knew my work. Mike Bollman and Dick Hayden were good friends of Ed Meyer. They listened as I presented my case to be a judge and explained how I would handle aspects of judging without sight. They listened and asked questions. They were convinced that I possessed the knowledge, experience, temperament, and character to be considered for appointment. Those three judges were part of the local committee which recommended potential judicial appointments to the Governor's Judicial Secretary.

In February 1998, I was asked to meet the Governor's Judicial Secretary at a law office in San Diego. We met for about an hour and discussed, in general terms, the role of judges and the philosophy of judging. I talked about my trial experiences, personal life, background, politics, and community work with veterans locally and nationally via the BVA. He knew I had support from the DA's office, many judges, veterans groups, disabled groups, and some judges who knew him personally.

On March 11, 1998, the Judicial Secretary to California Governor Pete Wilson, John Davies, called me at my office in the DA's offices and informed me that I was selected to be a judge on the Municipal Court. A public announcement would come out the next day, so he asked me to keep it private between Janice and me until it was public. I tried to call

Janice and could not track her down. When I arrived home from work, I found her, walked up to give her a hug and said, "I am a judge."

I was to be sworn in on March 12, 1998. It was twelve years and three days after my first day as a prosecutor. I was so very proud of myself and how far I had come from that bleak day in March twenty-nine years earlier.

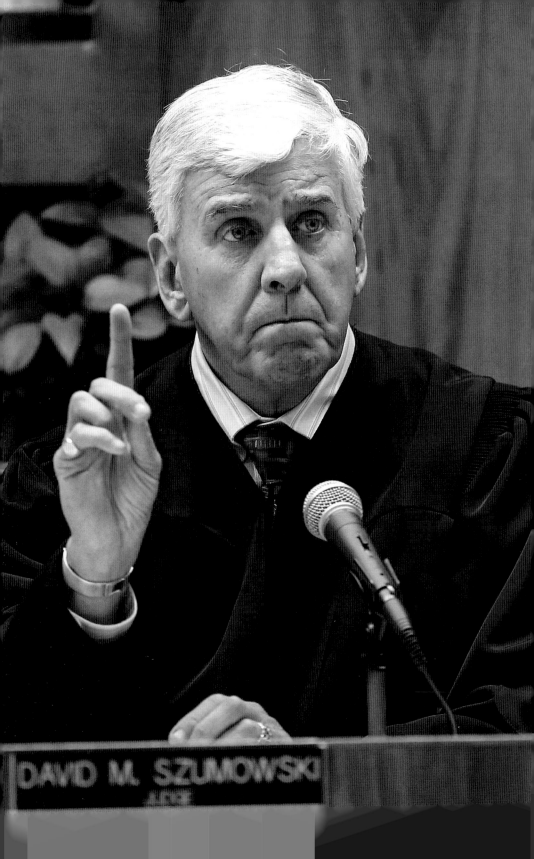
DAVID M. SZUMOWSKI
JUDGE

10

The Bench

We celebrated that evening, and I went to work the next day. I arranged to be sworn in at noon by the Presiding Municipal Court Judge John Davidson. Janice and just a few other court staff attended as I took the oath of office and transferred from the DA's payroll to the state's budget. I hosted a semi-formal swearing in for the judges, family, friends, and former prosecutors and defense attorneys on March 20, 1998. I chose that date purposely. It was on that date in 1969 that my life changed forever in Vietnam. I had come full circle from facing an uncertain future, to now having reached the high point of my career. It was a very emotional moment for me. It was also bitter sweet. Tom Christisen, my mentor and friend from my early law practice days, had been appointed to a judicial seat by Governor Wilson a couple of years earlier. I was appointed to fill the judicial seat which had been occupied by him. Tom had tragically passed away while on an anniversary trip in Europe. To be named to the seat of my friend was an honor.

I took a few days to clean out my old office and settle into my new court chambers. I would be an observer for a few weeks, and my mentor judge would help me get situated and the state began to send me reams of materials on various topics related to judging.

My selection as a judge was a surprise to most of the prosecutor's office. It was certainly a surprise to most of the court's judges and staff. Once again, I would be observed and evaluated as to my ability to handle the work. The same preparation skills, professionalism, listening skills, and fairness that I employed as a lawyer would now be the foundation for my judicial career. It didn't take very long for my colleagues to realize that I was a judge doing the work required albeit differently than was normal for them.

I began to interview from the pool of available court clerks and chose Sheri King. The San Diego Marshall's office provided court security, and I selected Chris Martinez as my bailiff. They did not have much to do while I was shadowing other judges, so they helped where they were needed.

The court was also providing me with a paralegal assistant to provide necessary sighted support for research, helping with exhibits for hearings, reviewing complaints and other court documents with me, and reading jury instructions to a jury. The search process took a few weeks, and I eventually offered the position to Patricia Johnson. She and I worked together for ten years before the nature of my work changed such that her skills and talents were being wasted by remaining with me.

All newly appointed and elected judges attend a new judge training workshop for one week in San Francisco. Pat and I attended, along with fifteen other new judges. The focus of the training was on sensitivity to people, ethics, diversity, role playing, and learning the exchange of function from advocate to impartial judge.

Later in the summer, Pat and I attended a two-week state-wide judge school held at the University of California on the Berkeley campus. There, we all attended class seminars taught by experienced judges on the various topics and disciplines within the law that required decision-making by judges. Nearly all subjects were given some exposure. They included probate, evidence, trials, appeals, jury instructions, juvenile law, dependency and delinquency, civil practice, traffic court, small claims matters, and criminal law. The time passed quickly during these sessions, and we were set up in small teams to do some role playing for a mock trial.

They fed us well, and we stayed in the dorms on campus. I took my dog Lucky with me, and he was the object of much attention. I was a unique presence in the training because I was the only blind person there.

The final night was festive with a banquet and skits from each team. Our team did a rendition of the Gladys Knight song "I Heard It Through The Grapevine." I stood behind the singer in our group doing the Pip thing-moving my hips and twirling my hands left and right to the music. We had a great time. After our skit, I spoke to the assembled audience and recited a poem I wrote. Since much of the training we received was a bit stiff at times, and the structure elicited sighs and eye rolls, I focused on the political correctness of the overall training and lampooned it. I got a rousing applause from about half of the audience and disappointed looks from some of the rest who, no doubt, were the instructors. I do have that devilish streak in me. I was never invited back to judge school.

Over the first eight months of my new job, I handled misdemeanor trials, preliminary hearings, suppression motions seeking to disallow seized evidence confiscated during a search by police, landlord tenant disputes, traffic court, misdemeanor arraignment court, and custody issues for arraignment of misdemeanor charges. I found that judging was interesting and fun for the most part. I had a dozen years of criminal experience that enabled me to slide into the new job easily.

California was voting that year on a consolidation referendum to join the municipal and superior court divisions into one entity known as the Superior Court. Every county would thus be consolidated under one state-wide court management system. There was local deference to the presiding judge of each county to run the county and make judicial assignments. The measure passed in November 1998 and in December, the Chief Justice of the Supreme Court of California came to San Diego to formally swear in all former municipal court judges as superior court judges. Even Lucky got to wear a dog robe that was crafted for him.

It was also in December of 1998 that my rotation turn in felony arraignment court was to begin.

Under the old municipal court rules, judges rotated into the various assignments known as moving departments. These were courts where volume was the key word and fast decisions the key element to making them work properly. I had done several, and felony arraignment was one of those courts. Judges would spend a month or two in these courts before going back to their home court, doing trials and assorted hearings. However, the rules of the Superior Court were different, and each judicial assignment was for one year. Certain assignments, such as juvenile or family court, could be two or three years. I was starting on Department 12, and it would be my assignment for all of 1999.

My initial responsibility in my court was to handle bail reviews, extraditions, further criminal proceedings, settle welfare fraud cases, and hear probation revocation cases. That was the morning work. The afternoon was devoted solely to arraignments. I would review my morning work with Pat Johnson in advance of court actually starting. I took braille notes where I needed them and managed to rule on most matters after hearing arguments from attorneys.

My staff consisted of my Clerk Sheri, my Bailiff Chris, and my Court Reporter Mindy Barlow. Everything was "on the record." Inmates were brought to court from the nearby jail, and their attorneys would argue for lower bail or actual release on a promise to appear for future court appearances. Over my eighteen years on the bench, I was not a big fan of trusting defendants to keep that promise, so bail was usually kept in place. It would cost them money to get out of jail, or they needed to post a bond.

I handled the extradition cases for our county. Often, a person was arrested in California on an arrest warrant issued by another state. My function was to insure that the warrant was proper, issued for a felony crime, and that the person before me was the correct person. Most of the time, a defendant waived extradition and agreed to return to the other state. However, he or she would remain in custody until authorities from the demanding state came to San Diego to take the person back. Some individuals were able to post bail and get out and return on their own to settle their legal issues in that state. The process was more complicated and time consuming if the person chose to fight the extradition process. In the long run, they usually lost the battle anyway and ended up being returned to the demanding state.

I presided over many hundreds of guilty pleas for the crime of welfare fraud and perjury. These cases were relatively easy to prove as I learned early in my prosecutorial career. I sentenced these defendants for probation grants. The goal was the restitution of the money, not jail time.

Most of my time was focused on hearing probation matters. I reviewed twenty or more cases a day which were set before me for some kind of ruling. Many involved a probationer alleged to have violated one or more of the terms of the probation grant. The hammer held over them was jail or prison time if they did not comply. The excuses for bad behavior were often stupid mistakes, but they could get creative at times, too.

I recall asking one defendant why he did not have a job so he could repay his fines and make restitution. His response was enlightening, "I have an aversion to work," he said. I looked at him for a long moment before inquiring, "And does that aversion also apply to jail?" His smirk disappeared quickly, and he began to nervously look to see if my bailiff was going to handcuff him. We discussed his realistic options, and I gave him time to find work and show me he was serious about staying out of jail.

Over the years, I found that most probation violations were due to people not taking the gift of probation seriously enough before realizing they could go to jail for a year or prison for several years. By definition, a probation case generally meant that the person made some judgment mistakes which violated the law. Most were not bad or evil people. Those people generally never had the probation opportunity; they went to prison. They were the violent defendants, such as molesters, armed robbers, murderers, and the like. Many were prior criminals and knew they were on the path of a life of crime and prison. I only saw these people in arraignment court. Their cases either settled with plea agreements in another court or went to trial for a jury determination of guilt or innocence.

Afternoons were reserved for arraignments. This was the defendant's first court appearance after being arrested. The Deputy District Attorney assigned to my court would represent the state and argue for bail based on the charges and prior record of the defendant. Most defendants were in custody, but some came to court after being notified by mail of pending charges. Others appeared after posting a bond after their arrest. If they were out of custody, they generally remained out so long as they continued to make their court appearances. The custody inmates were assigned a public defender to represent them until the case concluded. If they could afford to hire their own private attorney, they did.

My court always had an assigned public defender to assist with arraignments. This attorney and his interns would advise defendants of the charges, the bail, their Constitutional rights, get information about their personal life to help with the bail argument, and then enter not guilty pleas for them. My responsibility was to insure they understood the charges and their rights before setting bail and moving the case forward in the system toward a resolution or eventual trial.

This was the afternoon work for me daily for eighteen years. I probably presided over 200,000 cases where defendants were charged with one or more felonies, and I made rulings on more than twice that number of cases during my time on the bench.

The nature of my daily routine changed slightly over time. Eventually I transferred the welfare fraud cases to a regular disposition court. Soon, my experience and the routine nature of the work resulted in me not needing the total daily assistance of a full-time paralegal and some of Pat Johnson's time was devoted to other duties. She was reassigned to the family court as a facilitator until illness forced her to leave the court. I utilized other court staff for the hour or so I needed assistance with reading files and advising me of the things I needed to know during arraignments. This scheme worked well for the last six years of my work. I worked very well with Lisa MacMillan, Lori Brown, Yvonne Castro, Xochitl Lugo, and Ana Munoz. Dave Gonzalez was my trusty court reporter for the last years of my career. About fifteen people were involved in making my court run smoothly, and their experience and professionalism made me look good.

I was blessed with several wonderful clerks after Sheri moved out of state. Frances Mercer was professional and efficient for the two years she worked with me, before she wanted a change of pace regarding the court work. Chris Bermudes was my clerk for the next six years. Marcia Butcher took her place when her judge moved to a branch office in our county.

My last clerk, Michelle Knight, also known as Ms. Fix-it due to her ability to solve any problem, finished out my judicial career with me.

I utilized many deputies from the San Diego Sheriff's office as my bailiffs over the years. The men and women who handled these duties did so with skill, experience, dedication and professionalism. Their primary duty was to keep me safe during court sessions, control the court calendar and the spectators. My court was always very busy. At times, tension and tempers could run high. Crimes were serious and often the members of the public were present, distraught and angry if loved ones had been hurt or injured. Gang cases presented their own set of security issues for my bailiff.

Deputies Rich Bolter, Adrienne Candelore, Andrea Ladd, Steve Walling, Tony Valdez, Ed Southcott, Lily Lemos, and Gloria Barrera-Guijaro provided for my safety, professional control over all situations, and insured the efficient operation of my court. I was very fortunate to have such quality people working with me. I rarely needed to generate work for a secretary, but I was blessed to have Jocelynne Bower as my secretary until she retired, and then Jennifer McKee supported me until I retired. Jenny was a tremendous help following my retirement, too. As I wrote this autobiography, she proofed it and corrected many errors.

One of the many aspects of my work for the court was having the opportunity to speak to school children. Two or three times a week during the school year, children ranging from fourth grade to high school seniors would come to visit my court as part of a tour tied into their civics and government classes. I took time to explain how my court worked, what I did every day, and answered any questions they had. They were able to observe attorney arguments and hear defendants trying to explain to me why they were messing up their lives and in jail. Some of their questions were career oriented and many involved pointed questions about me, my blindness and how I got to be a judge. Invariably, someone always wanted to know how much I was paid. My standard answer was, "more than I deserve! You can Google it." In my career, I spoke with more than 32,000 students.

You might be wondering about the length of my tenure in arraignment court. I mentioned the fact that Superior Court judges held certain assignments for a year usually. Well, I happened to like the assignment I was given, and the work load was high volume. Most judges did not want that type of stress and tediousness. It suited my personality and temperament perfectly, so I volunteered to do it another year. The Presiding Judge was pleased because it removed the necessity of assigning someone who really did not want to do it. I learned in my time in the Army to never volunteer, but this time it felt right. As things turned out, the Presiding Judge did not have to make that assignment for 18 years. Department 12 was mine for the duration of my judicial career!

I stood for election three times during my career, and each time I ran for election I was not challenged. Thus, I never appeared on a ballot. I was very fortunate. In many counties in California, running for a judicial seat is blood sport, and many judges have to spend significant time and money politicking in order to convince the voters in their county to reelect them to a new six-year term. I'm grateful to the attorneys of San Diego County for not challenging me. I took this gesture as a mark of their respect for me, my judgment, and my fairness in the performance of my job. This respect and honor was shown years later when several hundred members of the bar and bench attended my retirement celebration.

I don't intend to bore readers with war stories, however there are some generalities that will give you a flavor for the work in my court. The arraignments were always very short appearances for defendants, but often the unstable defendants would go off on me, the system, the country, and the court's authority to make rulings concerning them. In those instances, after trying to calm them down with softer speech and concern for their views, I would have the bailiff escort the defendant from court. Some were clearly of dubious sound mind, so they received an eventual trip to the shrink for evaluation. Others just wanted to vent a little. Most of them wanted to simply get released from jail on their promise to appear. That did not happen often with me.

I have had some interesting characters appear before me. One defendant called me by my first name. I told him that he could not call me David as we were not friends. He didn't miss a beat and said "that's okay, Mr. David."

A female defendant stood before me in handcuffs. My trusty clerk whispered to me that she was very pregnant. So, thinking that fact might affect my decision, I inquired as to when the baby was due. She said, "Oh, Judge, I'm not pregnant. I'm just fat." I looked at my clerk who was red-faced as she slid lower into her chair.

I especially recall one defendant who was arrested for possessing drugs to sell. He claimed that California could not prosecute him since he had Inter Galactic Immunity. Naturally, this got everyone's attention. He proceeded to tell me that he was from the planet Monkey, and California had no jurisdiction to hold him. He went to see the shrink, too.

An English defendant insisted on referring to me as Your Lordship. I thought that had a nice ring to it.

A few defendants challenged my authority to judge them at all. They felt God was their only judge, and I was a mere mortal. I agreed that God would judge us all in time, but for now, he was busy trying to bring about peace in the world, and defendants were stuck with me. This usually got a few snickers from the audience.

I recall a trial I handled where the jury contained a fellow judge. I thought one side or the other would dismiss her but neither did. I used my computer with its speech program to take notes during the trial. I had an earphone jacked into it so only I could hear the speech feedback. After taking a break and checking on the World Series score, I reported to the trial participants the most recent score. The judge in the jury box inquired if I was really taking notes, or was I somehow just listening to the ball game during trial. Of course, that got some laughs.

I always enjoyed yanking the chain of defendants who cried poverty when I inquired about their not paying fines or making restitution. My clerk would whisper to me about the nice suit, fine hair styling, expensive purse or acrylic nails that various defendants displayed. When I pointed out these contradictions to their claim of being poor, their jaws dropped, they stammered, the audience chuckled, and I got the usual song and dance about everything was a gift.

One day while working in my office with my assistant, the door from the courtroom opened without a knock. No one ever entered without knocking. It was a female intern from the defender's office. I looked up and said "hello." She said, "Hi, I'm just going to use the rest room." Nobody uses my private rest room. It and a parking space were the perks of the job. Most judges even had a window in their office, and I didn't even have that. She came out of the rest room and said goodbye. My assistant and I sat with eyebrows raised throughout this incident. Before going back into court, I asked to see the supervising attorney for the interns. I explained what just happened, and he was suitably shocked. He thought she knew to use the employee rest room. He apologized and left. When I entered the court, there was one young intern with a very red face. She later apologized to me.

There is always some humor in even sad situations. One young defendant was in custody, and I was deciding how long to keep him there. I inquired as to his job situation, and he proceeded to tell me that he was a great cook and worked in a nearby restaurant. I knew of the place and asked him if the food was good. He said it was, and he offered to make me his specialty if I came in. He then reminded me that for him to do that, he would, of course, need to be out of jail.

Of course, not everything goes smoothly in court. Some defendants call me names. Others make crude remarks to the staff. One actually pushed down his jail pants and relieved himself on my carpet. That was one way to clear the courtroom!

I mentioned that many people don't view me as being without sight, especially after they get to know me and spend time with me. One day, I decided to do something out of the ordinary. A friend loaned me a pair of his wire rim glasses. I looked pretty distinguished when I tried them on, so I brought them to court one day and took the bench wearing them. The normal noise of my court suddenly subsided, and it got unusually quiet. I did my morning work and noted some hesitation by most of the lawyers before me. Finally, one brave soul simply asked, "Your Honor! Are we all witnesses to a miracle?" I removed the glasses, told them they were not seeing a miracle, and asked if they didn't think I looked good in glasses. That broke the ice, and most thought it was pretty funny.

The probation cases were the primary interest for me. These involved defendants who had been given a major break by being allowed to serve some jail time instead of years in prison. In exchange, they had to comply with various conditions of probation under the supervision of a probation officer. It baffled me to see how seemingly simple tasks and obligations were ignored to the point that the probationer would get rearrested by the probation officer and run the risk of me sending them to prison for years. I am talking about things like showing up for a meeting with probation, failing to drug test, failing to seek employment, failing to remain law abiding, and generally not complying with relevant conditions of their probation grant.

Defendants would admit the error of their ways and then the arguments would be made to persuade me as to punishment. I believe that in most cases, my decision was correct. However, I realized that these people were not necessarily bad or evil, but they were making bad judgment decisions which had adverse consequences for them. I tried to be fair, and I bent over backwards most of the time to show them there was a better alternative to seeing me.

I was rewarded on many occasions with a defendant's success. Some would come to court after probation to thank me for putting a fire under them. While walking the streets of San Diego at lunch time, often a defendant would say hello and thank me for helping him or her. These encounters made me feel like I was making a bit of a difference.

The Probation Department awarded me Judge of the Year recognition after I was on the bench three years. The District Attorney's Office honored me with the Judicial Excellence award shortly after I retired. I will cherish these honors as recognition from the community that I did my job well.

11

Technology

Technology has been a great assist to the blind community. We have come a long way from the stand alone Perkins Brailler and hand held slate and stylus for writing braille. While many still utilize these devices, the technology has progressed significantly in the last 45 years.

When first blinded, I was issued the brailler by the VA. I used it primarily to take notes at home during law school. I relied on a cassette tape recorder for class notes. Naturally, without sight, my handwriting began to deteriorate, although I tried to write from memory of the shapes of letters and how I used to write them. It soon became apparent that my writing was illegible. I would write larger, and the lines were not straight.

I began to use a typewriter, and it simplified my life greatly. It also made it much easier for those who had to read what I wrote. Soon, my initials became my signature and that was about the only handwriting I ever did thereafter.

I was also issued a Kurzweil reading machine. This was developed as an optical scanner and would read printed text and convert it to speech in a computerized voice which was actually quite easy to understand. The reader cost about $50,000, and it was purchased for me by the VA.

If you can recall the size of a reel to reel tape system, then you will understand what half of the reader was. One unit was the scanning camera, and the other unit was the computer processor. A single type-written page would take about four minutes to scan before it could be read aloud. I scanned many books with this device, and it would take many hours to finish scanning a book. The storage buffer was small, too, so when filled, I had to read what I scanned before I could scan more. Obviously, this was cumbersome.

The size of the scanner eventually got smaller and combined into one unit at half the price. It scanned pages faster, but still had limited buffer space. As before, I had to read what was scanned before continuing, or transfer it into my computer as a download.

Today, thankfully, the digital technology has made giant leaps forward with many aspects of audible recordings from scans. I now have a scanner camera that is about two inches by four inches and one inch thick. It is affixed to an arm which extends over a printed page and is connected to a speech program in my computer. By touching the space bar on the computer, I can alert the camera to take a picture of the page under it and in four seconds, the computer speech program starts reading. It does not read handwriting.

I can change some settings in the computer program and scan an entire printed book in just a few hours or less, depending on the length of the book. The program has a collating feature, so I can scan all odd numbered pages and, with a key stroke, scan the even numbered pages backward and, with another stroke, collate the material into proper reading order. This is a tremendous advance and time saver.

Much of my prosecutorial work was done with sighted help and braille notes. I used braille notes during my tenure as a judge, too. However, the digital advances in scanning and audible output have made my leisure reading life very easy and enjoyable.

Today, I also use a speech program on my PC, and I am able to access the Internet and mail programs with the speech program known as JAWS. I have been a JAWS user for about twenty years. It has undergone significant improvements to adapt to a fast changing technological world. Accessibility for the blind has been the motivation for the program changes over the years. Today, my speaking voice is a female, and she sounds very real. I can choose male or female voices, and there are speech programs in many languages.

The Library of Congress has always had a talking book division. Early books were recorded on wax disks, then vinyl and floppy disks. Now they are digital and downloadable directly into computers and other hand held devices. There is very little in the media that is not accessible to the blind whether audibly or with electronic braille devices.

The tools are available to allow all disabled people to succeed in most professions. The public needs awareness of a person's ability, not disability. Employers need to understand what people can do, not prejudge them as to what they cannot do.

I have read thousands of books audibly since I lost my sight. Reading is my favorite pastime. Today's technology makes it very easy to do. Many books are available commercially, and I use them in my hand held reading device, my phone with its voice-over component, Kindle, and Library of Congress apps. Podcasts are also downloadable to these devices. There is very little information available to the sighted world that is not also available to the blind community. While I rely on speech, many blind people rely on electronic devices that provide the same output in braille.

I started with a cane, went to using a dog, experimented briefly with a laser cane and hand-held electronic devices for travel. While interesting from a technological standpoint, in my opinion, nothing tops the joy and confidence I feel when traveling with a dog.

Machines can do wonderful things to assist the disabled. A trained animal can do similar wondrous things to enhance the life of a disabled person. Machines need care and maintenance and so does the assistance animal. However, when I feel a little blue, or just need some comfort, I get it from my dog, not a cane. I relish the responsibility that comes with a dog guide. He/she takes care of me, and I take care of him/her.

12

Love On The Left

Many things make one's life complete. Certainly, having a purpose in life is helpful. Most people want a decent job so they can care for themselves and a family.

I was fortunate in most respects. I eventually had a great career, met and married a wonderful woman with whom to spend my life, and was blessed to have found The Seeing Eye guide dog program.

Over the last 49 years, I have had six wonderful guide dog companions. They have brought safe travel, speed of movement, unrestricted love and companionship into my life. They have been conversation starters, relationship enhancers, and a calming presence in my life which has contributed to my good health, if for no other reason than the need to exercise them with long walks. They were always ready to go when I had to leave the house.

I never really understood why the vast majority of the blind community prefers a cane over a dog guide. I'm sure a good part of the reason is the lack of desire to care for someone/something other than oneself. Yes, there is a great responsibility when one has an animal. A guide dog is the eyes and ears of a blind person. They are trained for safety while walking, obedience to commands, intelligent disobedience if the command or situation presents danger, love and companionship. Contrary to popular belief, guide dogs are not trained to protect, although the natural instinct of some breeds will bring out that trait.

With all that a guide dog does for a blind person, there is an equal responsibility that flows to the dog also. The dog is a tool, but unlike the cane, it breathes, eats, sleeps, needs relief outings, care and love. This takes time and effort and perhaps many blind people don't wish to give what it takes to work with a dog.

Jon was my first dog. He and I learned together and experienced some growing pains. I was newly blinded and learning to cope with blindness, thinking about a future life, figuring out where that life would be located, and learning about caring for a dog. No doubt, I made mistakes along the way, but we soon learned to trust one another.

I arrived at The Seeing Eye guide dog school in Morristown, New Jersey, in late November 1969. My first instructor was Ramon Arenas. He showed me to my room where I met my roommate. He was there for his second or third guide dog.

The next morning after breakfast, I went with Ramon on a Juno walk. Juno is the name used for a trainer walk where the trainer acts as the dog and the trainee student holds the harness handle in the left hand. On this walk, the trainer asked about my daily routine, job or school, etc. We walked and talked, and he gaged my balance, my stride, and my pace. In his mind, he is trying to match those attributes of mine and my temperament to one of the many dogs he has trained which are ready for placement with a blind student. For me, he chose a male German Shepherd named Jon.

Jon was all black and 60 pounds of energy. It was love at first contact for me. I sat on the floor and petted, hugged, and played with Jon. He wanted no part of me and kept going to the door to go to Ramon. Eventually, he learned that I would not open the door, so he came and licked my face. That night at dinner, all students made their way using only a leash with their dog walking obediently at their left side, as they were trained to guide and heel on the left. Each student sat with their new dog at their side. Dinner was chaotic as the dogs would not stay in the down position. There were four trainers with about six students each. They told us that eating was second. Placing the dog in the proper down position came first. Eventually, calmness prevailed, and we managed to eat a colder meal.

The dogs were not yet in harness, so each student carefully, under the watchful eye of trainers, returned to the lounge area. We received instruction every day on a variety of topics from dog health, grooming, food, dog freedom off leash, dog proofing a home, dog senses, and good dog citizenship.

The training with harnessed dogs involved learning how to read the harness from the dog's movements. We began with inside work in hallways wide and narrow, turns into doorways with wide and narrow door jams, correct entry into areas through closed doors, correct entry into a vehicle, how to manage a revolving door, an elevator, an escalator, a cafeteria line, entry to a bus or train, and proper positioning of a dog on a plane.

We walked on streets and learned how to interpret dog signals for up and down steps, curbs, ramps at street corners, building overhangs, working through areas with tight quarters on streets or inside buildings, navigating and controlling the dog around a stray dog, working in a crowd of people, and, yes, even what to do when nature calls and the dog relieves itself on the sidewalk. Lesson one, always carry bags. Much time was devoted to working the dog in traffic situations on busy streets; cars; buses; and traffic at lights where cars are always moving. These were hectic times and potentially dangerous for both student and dog. Soon, I learned to trust Jon's training, and I gained confidence that he would not put either of us in a dangerous situation.

Jon became my eyes. I was 24 years old and in good shape. The speed of walk compared to cane use sold me on using a dog. Jon would be the first of six dogs I would have over the next 49 years as of this writing.

He and I experienced as many life situations as we could in the four weeks I was in training. He gradually stopped looking back at Ramon, and instead looked at me. He obeyed my commands of "left, right, forward, steady, hup hup, sit, rest and down." Jon slept next to my bed at night on a chain. He was always with me unless chained. By the end of a week, the chaos of the first day was nowhere in evidence. A blind stranger entering the dining hall would never know there were 24 dogs there.

Jon was a great companion as we walked through slush and snow that winter. We took a family trip to Mom's brother's place in Virginia. There, I had my first scare with Jon, because he was not tied to a bench correctly and decided to explore the area on his own. This was not a good situation. Guide dogs live in a very controlled environment and are not free to roam and get into trouble. Cars and garbage are the immediate danger, but, at my uncle's place, there were also copperhead snakes and farm animals nearby that Jon was not used to confronting. Eventually we found him after everyone went in all directions calling his name. Thereafter, I made sure he was secure.

Jon was with me during my move to Denver in 1970 to start a new life as a law student. We explored Denver, got situated with the school layout, and began a twelve-year relationship. Jon and I had great fun when he and I lived alone. He would often take me into the ladies rest room, which usually caused some commotion. In restaurants, we might end up in the kitchen at times. He was a magnet for women and children. Those twelve years also included personal struggles for me, moving to San Diego, and having a new person in the home when Janice moved to California. He was a hit at the VA for the three years I worked there. Then, age related issues caught up with him, and he had great difficulty walking. I had to let him go to his reward.

The big guy, OJ, came into my life in 1982. He was a majestic German Shepherd. He had great energy and was always ready for anything. When he entered my life, Janice and I were having difficulties, and I relocated to downtown San Diego after we separated. OJ and I lived in an apartment, and we walked to our job with the VVLP (Vietnam Veterans Leadership Program) several blocks from our apartment. He was part of the face of the program as we met civic leaders, business leaders, veterans groups, and involved ourselves with projects and programs to promote Vietnam veterans in business.

I was also active with the BVA nationally, and he and I made several cross country trips to veterans meetings in Washington, DC. I'm not sure his nearly 90 pounds would fit under the seat in today's cramped airplanes. But then, he could fit. He was a handsome dog and caught the eye of many a flight attendant who felt badly about his being so squeezed in those seats. There were many flights where he and I would get bumped to first class with all the perks that went with the status.

OJ transitioned with me from VVLP to solo practice in the law firm. Unfortunately, his good looks did not result in business for me. He became an official legal "beagle" when I became a prosecutor with the DA in San Diego. He was always well-mannered in the office and in court. He could always break the tension of a trial with snores, or little yelps, as he had dog dreams while snoozing.

I remember one trial I had in the South Bay. I had been there nearly a year and had been in a certain court many times. The judge was a nice older man whom most of us found quite funny at times. Well, I need to say at this point that most people who would look at me would not know initially that I could not see. I had two prostheses which looked like real eyes, and I had good eye muscle control. I also took my own notes in Braille, so I carried sheets of paper filled with many dots. During one trial with this judge, I was making a closing argument to a jury. I heard the judge whisper to his clerk, "There isn't any writing on his notes." The clerk, with complete calm and poise, said in a whisper, "Your Honor, Mr. Szumowski is blind and his notes are in Braille." The judge then whispered to his clerk, "Oh, then that must be why he brings his dog everywhere."

I could hear the whispers, and I can only imagine what the jury may have heard. There were many experiences over my life when people meeting me were not quite sure of my sight impairment but nearly all knew that the dog was a guide dog.

OJ was with me for about eleven years, and he developed the same hind quarter, hip issues that befell Jon. I retired OJ to be a house dog and returned to The Seeing Eye to obtain dog number three, Lucky, my third male shepherd.

Lucky was the typical shepherd with some white markings. He was young and active. He got along well with OJ, but OJ could not run with him due to the leg issues. After about a year, it was time to let OJ go to his reward. Lucky was the trial dog. He made his presence known in court and the office by talking in his sleep. He was a solid companion, and I walked all over Coronado with him. He would go to the beach and romp in the surf while tied to an extension leash. He loved the ocean. Of course, cleaning him up after the salt bath was a chore.

Janice and I were now living in our new house, and we had three birds now. Lucky did not seem to be all that interested in the birds, fortunately. One day, I noticed a soft lump on one of Lucky's toes. When he was examined by a vet, we discovered that he had an aggressive form of cancer. He eventually had the toe amputated, and it didn't seem to slow him down.

Our home was burglarized one evening when we forgot to set the alarm. Fortunately, Lucky was alert enough to hear the downstairs intruders, started barking, and tore down stairs after them. The burglars did not get away with much, but that incident changed Lucky to being more aggressive. Aggression is not bred into guide dogs. They go to many public places, and they cannot be feared by the public. Dogs showing aggressive tendencies during their training do not become guide dogs.

This was about the time when I moved from being a prosecutor to a judge. I was sworn in as a judge with Lucky at my side. During court proceedings, often attorneys will need to come to talk with me at the side of the bench. This sudden appearance by lawyers began to startle Lucky. He did not see them approach, and he showed his displeasure by growling. Most people in the court thought it was funny, but I knew it was not acceptable, and it would be difficult to break. I began to consider retiring him after only eight years of service.

The decision was made for me one day when he was acting strangely and retching without throwing up much. He was ten, and we took him to the vet. The vet said he had flipped his stomach, and he was shutting down. I made the decision to let his suffering stop. Emergency surgery might have saved him, but he would have had damaged organs because of blood loss to them.

I went on leave from the court to obtain my first lab and my first female, Oakley. She was all black, but her feet were white. She weighed about 59 pounds, and she was as strong a dog as I had handled. She pulled so hard, I had a trainer come to help me figure out how to slow her down. To this day, I attribute my sore left shoulder to those years with Oakley. She was cute and so playful. Janice took to her more so than the other dogs. Our bird Smokey had learned the names of OJ and Lucky, and now learned to say Oakley, too. Of course, both Boo and Smokey could say Jan or Dave.

Oakley was a perfect lady everywhere she went. She would run around the house, and, if I was sitting on the floor, she would put her head down and do a somersault right into my chest with hind legs pumping. She gave me about ten years of excellent love, companionship and service. The stress of being in a busy downtown environment with lots of people and traffic took its toll on Oakley, and she began to slow down considerably. She also had cancer on her tail, and half of her tail was removed to prevent its spread. By now, electric cars were part of the traffic scene, and their quietness added stress to the dog's work. It got to a point where she was just too slow for my needs. I retired her, and she became Janice's dog. It is difficult to watch the dog that looked to me for her every need, suddenly wondering why I no longer attended to her. She would just look at me with sad eyes and seemingly ask "why?"

Soon though, she started hanging close to Janice and found that her needs were being met by another. She knew I relied on another when I returned home with my fifth dog, Kenny, a male Yellow Lab. Sadly, about two years after retiring Oakley, she suddenly collapsed while walking with Janice. Her trachea had collapsed, and she could not breathe. She died on the way to the vet.

In 2010, Kenny the licker entered my life. During training with him, I was listening to a lecture one evening when suddenly Kenny just crawled up into my lap during the lecture. The speaker stopped talking and said, "David, that is very cute and obviously Kenny likes you, but dogs belong on the floor, not your lap." I knew then that Kenny was going to be the most fun dog of all five. And he was. He always had his tail wagging and was ready to lick anyone who got close. He was a wonderful guide dog, too. I always referred to him as being on Kenny time, however. Getting from one place to another was time consuming because Kenny took his own sweet time walking. I sought the help of a trainer who came to my home to help figure out why he was slow. He, too, was baffled about why Kenny was not that energetic when it was not noted during his training.

Then, after having Kenny about a year or so, I noted a huge lump in the crook of his neck. There was one on either side of his chest bone. The vet took a biopsy and sure enough, the news was not good. He had lymphoma. We saw a cancer specialist, and we started Kenny on a regimen of expensive treatment. The Doc did not sugar-coat anything. He said this may work to shrink the lymph nodes, but it won't cure him. Eventually, it would kill him. We did the treatments, and he responded well for a time, but the doses also increased. They took a toll on his health. He continued to be slow and lacked interest. One day, shortly after my hip replacement surgery in December of 2012, I could tell Kenny was not focused or eating. We took him to the vet, and he told us it was time. It was about eleven months after I discovered the lumps. Janice and I got on the floor, stroked him and cried as the vet euthanized him He was only four years old. That was the fifth time I had lost a trusted loving companion. It was never easy, but as most of us know, the animals in our lives do not usually outlive us.

Two months later, I went to Morristown again and trained with my current stoic and healthy male Golden Retriever Speedwell. Speedwell is a beautiful Golden. He weighs about 75 pounds, and he is a perfect dog for my needs. He never barks, other than dog barks during sleep. He has an excellent pace for my aging bones. He was never rude in court except to sigh heavily as court dragged on close to lunch time. He is totally aloof to other people, cats and dogs. He is a perfect gentleman. I could rename him Shadow, since he is never more than about three feet from me at any time I am at work or home. He is usually walking around with a soft squeaky toy in his mouth. Judging guide work, manners, obedience, temperament, and general companionship, I might have to give the nod to Speed as perhaps the best of the six dogs.

This accolade was in doubt early however. Once I returned home from training with him, something shook his confidence in his work with me. He would not leave the sidewalk at my house. He refused commands and just wanted to go inside. I consulted the training staff, and we decided to leave him at home until his trainer could come to work with us. In about two weeks, Chris Mattoon came to our home and for the next four days, he tried to figure out why Speedwell would not work.

After two days, he was ready to suggest that I make a change. He tried one more day, and he walked with Speedwell but without me. They walked for hours and eventually Speedwell responded to Chris. I learned a collar technique to help get him started when he balked at moving. Once Speedwell knew that I knew that trick, he began to respond to me. Chris stayed another day to go to work with me, and we worked in the court and on the downtown streets. Thankfully, Speedwell and I both regained our trust and confidence in each other. There have been no other issues with him.

At this writing, he is seven and will have three to five more good years of faithful, loving service. Chris Mattoon has visited us a few times when he came to California on other business. He stayed with us, and, each time, it only took about fifteen seconds for Speedwell to detect his scent in our home and go crazy when he spotted Chris.

I am now at the age when the serious question of getting another dog begins to be relevant. The Seeing Eye will always allow former graduates to return for a new dog as long as their health can endure the training regime. I am fairly confident I will outlive Speedwell, but if he lives to his projected working life age of eight to ten years, then I will be in my mid-70s. If I am in good health and active still, I will likely go for number seven. I have decided that if I am not able to walk well enough to go places and keep the dog busy, then it would be unfair to take a well-trained guide dog and essentially make it a mere pet. I will cross that bridge when I need to.

Epilogue

Reflections

It was 2016. I had been thinking about retiring as I neared my 70th birthday in 2015. I had purchased my military time, which accelerated the time at which I would qualify for my judicial pension after 20 years of combined military and bench service. Of course, I did not have to retire because I had been reelected for a term which ran through 2020.

However, after 18 years of primarily doing the same work day in and day out, I was beginning to get restless. I was ready for something less tedious. I wanted to travel more while Janice and I had good health. I wanted to work on this autobiography in the hope that others might find inspiration from my life story. I also wanted to become more fluent in Spanish. I had been a golfer for many years, and I wanted to play more and lower my handicap. I enjoyed golf mainly because it was one sport which I could play. Team sports which required movement and vision were no longer options for me after Vietnam. Golf is a slower paced individual game. Sure, I needed some sighted help with my setup, direction, and club placement behind the ball, but after that, the swing tempo, muscle memory, technique and result were totally up to me. I have a pretty good sense of feel for the way the club hits the ball and the sound it makes. I know when it is a clean hit or not, and usually can tell the direction of the ball. Bunker work is something that needs professional help now and then. Ron Riess is a golf pro who has helped me over the years with troublesome aspects of my game. I am grateful to him for that help.

I rarely swing and miss the tee or approach shots, but when I do, I just smile and remind myself to lower my expectations. My irons need practice as does my chipping and pitching. I am a fairly good putter however, as long as my playing buddies can read the greens for breaks, distance and slope. Win or lose, golf is a great deal of fun for me and gets me out of the house seven or eight times a month. I have learned to never take myself too seriously when playing golf. I'm grateful to the several friends, especially George Beall, Joe Kampp, Pat Russell, Dan Lamborn, Genaro

Ramirez, Jim Goodwin, Dan Williams, Mike Carleton and Tony Valdez who have been willing to play with and help me. Golf is fickle. One day, many parts of my game click. Another day, only some or none click. That is secondary to the comradery that comes with golfing with friends on beautiful California days.

Once a year, I travel to Florida in the spring to meet my Phi Kap brothers and reminisce about our college days, play several rounds of golf over a few days, watch college basketball tournament finals, drink beer and tell lies about how good-looking we still are. It has been a great male bonding week for us, and we hope to keep it going as long as we are able. Richard Sinclair, Don Casper, Emmett Morgan, Frank Frye, and John Miller are great friends to have. Thank you all for being there for me.

Janice and I have been excellent financial managers and feel very secure with our retirement needs being met. Our pensions will keep us out of poverty and allow us to enjoy life with travel, etc.

Over the years we had become cruisers. We have traveled to Alaska twice, Hawaii twice, the Baltic Sea to visit Russia and some Scandinavian countries, the Caribbean to include a trip through the Panama Canal, South America for a trip around the southern tip of that continent, and a combined 35th anniversary/retirement trip to New Zealand and on to Australia. It is safe to say that we like cruising. We have taken a church trip to the Holy Land, visiting Israel and Jordan. Most recently, we took a wonderful land tour of Poland, Hungary, Austria, and the Czech Republic. I had always wanted to visit my grandfather's homeland.

We have met many interesting people on these trips, and they were from different areas of the world. We never took my dog. While guide dogs are allowed on cruise ships, the ship is confining. Taking the dog off the ship in foreign ports was at best risky. It also was not much of a vacation to get up early to tend to a dog's needs, nor was it convenient to take the dog on the excursion packages offered in the many destinations. So, the dog remained in his or her familiar home environment watched over and cared for by my secretary Jocelynne Bower or a close family friend, Stephanie Akerstrom, on the other occasions.

Now it is time to find new travel adventures. With the world in such turmoil, we think seeing some of America is a good place to begin. We live within two hours of a small desert town east of San Diego. Janice and I have enjoyed renting a duplex in Borrego Springs every year for the past thirty years. We enjoy the dry heat of the desert, the beautiful surrounding mountains, and the solitude that comes with the peacefulness of the desert.

I enjoy reading and have scores of books to read using a device which stores them in recorded format. My interests are primarily thriller and mystery novels and history, but I can be lured into a sci-fi book now and then. I am taking an interest in biographies, and novels off the best seller lists. There is so much information available now on computers and the internet that significant learning through speech and audio materials allows for little idle time. I am blessed with reasonably good health. Sure, there is arthritis which I can control and I've had new hips on both sides. But, I am hopeful that the entry into my declining years will be uneventful and the journey long. Now I have time to reflect on a variety of things that have occurred in my life.

People say hindsight is 20-20. I suppose that is true. I began to see things in life with more clarity as I got older. I have never thought of myself as very religious. I had that experience before going to Vietnam, when I felt the need to go to confession. I know I prayed while waiting in my tank to be rescued, but cannot honestly say I recall praying after I knew I would live. I'm sure I did at times.

Little did I know of the suffering and discouragement I would endure in coming years. I suppose there was an inner strength that helped me through the low periods. I can't say that it was my faith in God, because God and I were on the outs then, or at least I thought we were. Eventually I came to realize that God never gave up on me. When I understood this, I think I gained some wisdom about suffering and struggle. My perseverance and the support of family and friends helped me to understand that I had a life and could make a difference. I thank God for the path I chose, and the strength he gave me to pursue this life.

Janice and I recently traveled to eastern Europe. I had never been to Europe, and this trip included Poland. I reflected on Pop's upbringing as I knew it before he left Poland. He lived in a very small farming village in Poland which is now part of Ukraine. Some of his family was already in America. When it was his turn, he ventured forth as a teenager knowing only the Polish language. He arrived at Ellis Island and waited his turn. He found work as a laborer and got by in the Polish community. He earned enough money to live on while learning to speak English and make a better life for himself. He eventually married and had three children. Polish was the language of the house, and the children knew only Polish when they entered the school system.

I thought of his early life as I toured Poland and spoke with tour guides and some local people who spoke English. Pop left before World War I and the subsequent horrors of World War II and post war Communism. He was fortunate to be able to leave when he did. He struggled and survived.

When a medical tragedy struck Pop's wife, he was not able to care for all three children while she was hospitalized. My Dad and Nestor's Mom lived for several years with Pop's sister. It was only when Dad's mother died and Pop remarried Granny that the whole family was again reunited in the 1930s.

Pop and Dad both endured hardship and struggle. I thought about that character trait as I learned about the old country. I'm confident that their ability to endure hardship came through in my genes and helped me come out on top also.

This book is about my life. However, it is a story that really takes on meaning as a result of the Vietnam war. It changed the course of my life. As I have matured and made a life for myself, I have not spent much time dwelling on that war. Now, I have had time to think about the war and read many viewpoints on our involvement there. It seems clear now that we should not have gone into Vietnam. The Johnson administration never informed Congress about the true nature of developments in Vietnam. The funneling of more and more men and material into the fight was not making a positive difference. The American people were kept in the dark about progress there until the war started to play on nightly television news. Then, Americans woke up to the reality of our big mistake.

As a soldier sworn to defend the Constitution and obey lawful orders, I did not give much thought to evaluating the Vietnam War at the time. I did my duty until injured and retired. I am proud of my service and wish I had not been blinded, but as my life has turned out, I landed on my feet and would not change anything.

My goal was to write this book for myself and not necessarily for public consumption. I've had an interesting life following a serious setback. Maybe it is a story others would find inspiring or at least interesting.

I will play golf as often as I can. Janice and I will travel as we desire. I will try to stay physically fit with exercise, long dog walks, good eating habits, and taking care not to over indulge on anything.

My parents died too young. I have other relatives who lived well into their 80s. I hope those longevity genes are with me, too. However, I am comfortable with my faith in God and my eternal salvation through the grace of Jesus Christ. I like the Episcopal Church we attend.

I can't say that my faith has always been strong. Following my injury in Vietnam, I wondered why God picked me to bear the struggle. I drifted from my Catholic roots during college and while in the Army, but I remember going to confession after receiving orders to Vietnam. I simply felt that I needed to be right with God as I was heading off to war.

As I struggled with accepting blindness following law school, I was angry with God for quite a while. I did not attend church. As things got better in my life, I did slowly drift back to my faith. Janice and I settled on the local Episcopal Church as the place where we felt most comfortable. Edward Harrison was the Priest who forced me to confront my faith. He asked me to talk to a forum of parishioners about religion in my life after Vietnam. I had to give serious thought to my speech to the church assembly. It was that exercise that forced me to come to grips with my values, my roots, my emotions, and my perspective on the important things in life. I began to understand faith as a power greater than self. (see page 132)

I also realized that being angry with God was foolish. God did not care if I was angry with him. Through his son Jesus Christ, he loved me and would always love me. I realized that it was my subconscious awareness of Him that required me to ask for forgiveness for not keeping my faith in Him.

I could have been killed, and I wasn't. I could have given up on everything and just drifted through life, and I didn't. I could have settled for less, and I didn't. I deserted God, but he did not desert me. Wisdom comes slowly to some of us, but when it does, you know God had His hand in your awakening.

Law school gave me something positive to do as I slowly learned to heal from my trauma and learn to live my life differently. Family and friends were there to encourage me during the years of my struggles with the post traumatic stress I denied having. My first job with the VA helped me understand that I could be productive in spite of my disability. The Blinded Veterans Association and the VVLP gave me the confidence to interact socially in all situations without thinking that I was different from others. The job as a prosecutor reinforced my convictions that I was on a par with non-disabled lawyers. Finally, the acceptance of my peers in the law office and on the bench gave me the satisfaction in knowing that I was an equal.

I thank God every day for my life, my wife's love, my country for taking care of my needs after serving her, my supportive and loving family, my loyal friends, my satisfying career, my loyal and loving dogs, and especially for my good health. I am grateful for being able to find the courage to pursue my goals and persevere through the many challenges. I've tried to make the most of the opportunities given to me. I am by no means a perfect individual. I have made mistakes in life, both personally and professionally. I have learned from my mistakes. My goal now is to find peace and contentment in my time left on Earth, and trust in God's grace when my time to be judged arrives. I hope to show love and kindness to family and friends. I hope that my life has in some small measure contributed to making this community a better place.

I have not always been the easiest person to be around or with whom to live, so I ask for those whom I have offended or treated disrespectfully to find forgiveness in their hearts. I could not have achieved the success and contentment I have enjoyed without the loving support of Janice, my family and friends, and the unconditional love and the companionship of my dogs. I also want to acknowledge the memory of Edwin L. Miller, the District Attorney of San Diego. He took a chance when he hired a blind attorney, and I will be forever grateful for his having faith and confidence in me. He gave me the opportunity that allowed me to walk in the steps of my Grandfather, Pop, who undertook the challenge to leave his family as a teenager, cross an ocean, and come to a new land without speaking the language. He had few possessions, worked hard, and raised a family which now is in its fourth generation. We continue to strive and reach for more.

The End

Silver Star Citation

GENERAL ORDERS:

Headquarters, II Field Force Vietnam, General Orders No. 1485 (June 14, 1969)

CITATION:

The President of the United States of America, authorized by Act of Congress July 9, 1918 (amended by an act of July 25, 1963), takes pleasure in presenting the Silver Star to First Lieutenant (Armor) David M. Szumowski (ASN:)-5247367), United States Army, for gallantry in action while engaged in military operations involving conflict with an armed hostile force on 20 March 1969 while serving as a Platoon Leader with Company M, 3d Squadron, 11th Armored Cavalry Regiment, in the Republic of Vietnam. On this date Lieutenant Szumowski's platoon was the lead element in a combined force of tanks and armored cavalry assault vehicles during an assault on a well-entrenched enemy force. Disregarding the intense hostile small arms, automatic weapons and rocket propelled grenade fire, he assumed a fully exposed position upon his vehicle in order to effectively direct the assault on the hostile positions. As the friendly force advanced, Lieutenant Szumowski's tank sustained a direct hit, and he received severe fragmentation wounds leaving him totally blind. Nevertheless, he refused medical attention and remained in his vehicle in order to continue directing the assault on the enemy fortifications. Only after his platoon had made a complete sweep through the enemy base camp, inflicting severe casualties upon the enemy elements and destroying a number of enemy fortifications, did he consent to his evacuation. First Lieutenant Szumowski's outstanding courage and dedication to duty were in keeping with the highest traditions of the military service and reflect great credit upon himself, his unit and the United States Army.

Testimonial to Faith

(Audio Transcription)

Thank you all for coming. I'm very honored actually that you would take the time and hope that you find this time is of some value to you. When Edward asked me to do this, as he indicated in church this morning, I was a little hesitant to do it. I don't normally talk about myself, but I got to thinking about this and losing a little sleep over the last few weeks and rehearsed about five times, and every time has been different. So I've pared it down to about an hour and 47 minutes so (laughing) ten o'clock service will run until eleven. To talk about my life in 30 to 45 minutes will be difficult, but I'm going to try to hit the highlights.

I grew up in upstate New York. I was the son of two parents who both served in World War II. My Mother was a nurse. My Dad was a tank mechanic and I was the oldest of my generation — I was the first of my generation to go to college which was, I guess, a big deal to them. In hindsight I guess it was a big deal to me too, but at the time I didn't think much about it. I had a normal upbringing in a little town in upstate New York — population maybe of 20,000 people — graduating high school class of 195, so that was small. I was born and raised Catholic and I probably didn't go to church every Sunday, but I do recall going often even when I didn't want to, because my Dad was pretty firm about things like that. As I got to be older and a teenager, I often wondered about the wisdom of going to confession every Saturday night, knowing I would just be there the next week saying the same things over and over again, about how sorry I was for doing it again. (Laughter) Whatever it was. But I was a good kid, I think basically. I never got into trouble and then I went away to college. So I'm not going to talk about the growing up years anymore. That's not really all that interesting.

I went away to college and I would say probably my spiritual vacation began. As I've talked to others through life, many young people tend to drift from some of the things that parents force them to do or instill certain values when you're young — you don't know any better than to challenge them until you can get away when the leash isn't on you anymore. So I started to drift a little, but understand that I never didn't believe in God — I never had really serious doubts about heaven and life hereafter. College was a time for learning, fun, growing up, experimenting with a lot of different things — I don't mean drugs or anything like that — but alcohol flowed freely on the campus. For sure. I went to a Baptist school, so I did get my dose of religion through the monthly or bi-monthly convocations that we had to attend. I had to take a Bible class in school and that was a requirement to graduate — so I wasn't that far away from it.

I was in ROTC which is the way I ended up going into the service. I was commissioned as a second lieutenant in the Army. I did well in college with grades. I did well in the summer camp, so I had my choice of branch of service and I thought at that time that I might want to be a career soldier, so I picked a combat branch because even then we knew that the way to advance in rank was to be getting shot at if there was a war. So I picked the Army figuring okay — I wasn't really up on walking a lot. I thought riding would be good, and so I went to Fort Knox for training with tanks and thought I would be — uh you know, six inches of steel in front of me, that's pretty good too. And of course the Vietnam War was going at this time. I graduated in 1967 from college and went into the service.

So after a little stint at Fort Knox I got my orders to Vietnam, and interestingly enough, while I wasn't an active participant in religion, shall we say, through those years, I remember distinctly going to confession the last weekend I was at Fort Knox knowing that I was about to head overseas. So I guess something from my youth stuck — either that or I was darned afraid, and I wanted things to be right with God. I can't honestly say that I remember going to the mass, but I do remember going to confession.

I ended up over in Vietnam. I wasn't there very long. I was there about 40 days when a rocket grenade hit my tank and I would say fortunately for me, the guy was not a very good shot because had he hit where he was aiming and done serious damage, I might not be here today. But fragments caught my face and eyes and I was left blinded. And that was the end of my military career, and that was in March of 1969, so I'm coming up on 44 years of being blind…and that's a term I don't have any hardship about today — we get politically correct and it's "visually impaired, visually challenged, sightless"…you know. Whatever.

Now those things — that's the before, and now we're at the after: Life as a blind person. This is a new challenge obviously. My parents always held out hope that some miracle would come along; my eyes would settle down; that surgery could do something for me. I think the doctors didn't want to lay anymore stress on me than necessary at the time so they said, "You know, you need to give this some time. Go to rehab, learn how to do things without sight and let's take another look in five years." Well, later on, obviously I realized that they were — they knew what was in store for me but they didn't want to tell me then. So I took my time through Walter Reed getting out of the service, but I had a lot of fun in Washington. There really wasn't much they were doing for me medically, so I got a lot of convalescent leave and a lot of passes, and I was single, lot of women in Washington. My buddies and I, we lived all in one ward there, where the orthopedic guys were crazy on the other side of the hall, and all the visual guys were with me, and we made the best of it. We used to have back rub contests with all the student nurses. (Laughter) A dozen roses and a free meal at the mess hall of their choice to the winner. We knew on day one who the winner was — we dragged it out for about a month. So there were some fun times.

But then I got out and I went to the VA Hospital system — not at Walter Reed but at Hines, Illinois, and I learned how to do things without sight. I had an attitude. Some people still think I have an attitude. But I thought some of the things I had to do were just downright stupid. I knew how to type from high school, but they made me take typing. But I was good enough that I actually graduated using the electric typewriter. Yeah. No computers back in 1969. So I took typing, I learned how to read Braille. I still don't read it fast, people born blind will read Braille ten times faster than I would. I learned orientation which is cane travel, that was a big part of most every day for the 13 weeks I was there.

It was a 16-week program and I hated it so much I got out in 13 because I just wanted to be done.

I had to take shop. And I thought okay they handed me a bunch of leather with little holes in it and a string of plastic stuff that we called gimp when I was growing up, and I had to make a wallet. And I thought, what I am doing this for? I did that so well, they told me okay now you can sit over here at the loom and make a rug. That was a little more challenging with all these strings going up and down with different colored threads going through — umm. And then I graduated to making a foot stool, which actually was kind of fun because my Dad was pretty handy with tools, so I knew how to use saws and hammers and nails and screws and things like that, so I made a nice stool. And then I got onto a lathe which was a little more interesting. And I made a lamp. And I liked it so well I made a second one. I think I still have those — right? [Janice: Both!] Yes, got them both. So that was fun, to some extent.

And for recreation, I know everyone wants me to talk about golf — the recreation was to go out and hit golf balls in the net. That was one thing. I had played a little bit in college, not on the team, but just played golf and so I knew what I was doing. And it became more of an anger management opportunity for me. Whacking the heck out of a golf ball, knowing that I'm not going to hurt anybody except maybe myself if I swung and missed. Ah, and I always looked for opportunities to — I say I — all of us were young Vietnam blinded Vets there — always looking for opportunities to figure out how to get out of the hospital and go out on the town. Maywood, Illinois, was not a thriving metropolis, but the Lemon Drop Inn was the place to go. (Laughter) And we used to sneak over there and women were lying in wait for the blind guys to come. Because they get you out on the dance floor without our canes and then they wouldn't take you back to your chair. So we kept dancing and dancing and the beer kept getting warmer and warmer so finally we decided that we needed some other options here. And I won't go into any more of that.

I tried to make the best of 12 or 13 weeks there. I learned very quickly that you needed to distinguish between the tube of tooth paste and Ben Gay. (Laughter) My teeth never hurt, though! No, once is enough. Some say that when you lose one of your senses, the others pick up. And I think that's true. My sense of touch is certainly developed a lot more. Although Janice will strongly disagree, my sense of hearing is very good. (Laughter) But guys and gals, you know there is a difference between hearing and listening, and we all do selective listening, right?

I'm obviously more careful than I might be if I could see. I'm much more attentive to my surroundings than I was back then. I was very good with a cane, if I do say so myself. I was trying to set a speed record, until one day on a long trek I met a parking meter and my shoulder still hurts. But they don't give, so I learned to be a little bit more humble. Some of the volunteers would come and visit the guys on the weekend and take us out for walks and I guess then I had an attitude, I didn't want any help, I could do this myself, and blah blah blah. And so while walking through the park, I just kind of pulled my arm away from the gal that I was with. So I walked about 10 feet and a tree branch caught me right in the face and I went flat on my back. And she just leaned over and said, "You still want to do this by yourself?" So I learned. I learned. It's not always that easy.

I then had to figure out what I was going to do. I had VA benefits which were good, so I applied to law school and got into Denver University Law School, and between rehab and the following September when law school started, I had about six months of visiting my parents and my brothers and going back to my college campus and hanging out with some of my buddies. I was basically a bum, not knowing where to land, but I didn't want to stay in Gloversville. I told you it was a small town and there really wasn't much to do.

One of the first things I did after leaving the VA, and I said I was good with a cane, is I went right away and got a dog. Much to the annoyance of the VA people because they knew I knew what I was doing with a cane. But you had to know what you were doing with a cane even before you got a dog. In 1969 I got my first of five dogs — Jon, and I've had dogs ever since. You have to think a lot when you walk with a cane, you are obviously slower when walking. A dog eliminates a whole lot of distractions and things that might be obstacles you just don't even know about. As most of you know, I just lost Kenny about a month or so ago to cancer and I'm probably going to get number six here next month, in March maybe. But I learned quickly that walking down the hall at the courthouse there are signs in the hall that say "careful wet floor" — I've wiped them out like dominoes — never even knew they were there. And the cleaning crews are having a great time. "Go ahead go left go right — stop stop!" I try to get in early enough to just avoid all that.

But I got my dogs and that was a lot of fun. I've had a lot of fun experiences with the dogs. They always tell you to follow the dog, so I do and sometimes in restaurants I end up in the kitchen. (Laughter) I've been in more than one ladies room, ummm, but you don't have to worry because I'm not going to look — it's okay. And fun experiences with elevators — women I wish when you are standing by the buttons at the elevator you would say something if you see me reaching because if you don't, you know — I might hit where I shouldn't be hitting. That's every embarrassing. Um, the first time I went out for Mexican food after being blind, I sat down at the table and put my napkin in my lap and asked my date at the time, "Why is this napkin so hot?" And she said because it's your tortilla. (Laughter) So I had flour all over my pants, but I did the natural thing — I just ate my napkin. And yes, blind people do eat more lemon wedges and parsley than sighted people, in case you were wondering. It's just a given. We do that.

So I went to law school, finished it in normal time, took the bar and passed it in Colorado, and then I would say a steep slope faced me and I didn't know it. This is when I started to think more about my relationship with God and whether I was going to be angry with him and I think I was. I didn't have very good luck trying to find a job. It seems like a lot of doors were closed, whether it was because of me or because of the disability — I tend to think it was the disability at the time. But a lot of negative things started to happen. I would get depressed. I developed some bad habits. For sure I probably drank too much back then. And that leads to other changes in the way you perceive life. You sleep too late, you sleep at the wrong time, day becomes night, night becomes day. You wallow in self-pity which is what I was doing and it took me about, unfortunately, three years of lost time to figure out that crawling around in the bottom of the barrel was not the way that I should spend the next 30, 40, 50 years of my life. I was still young — I was mid-20s or so — and so I just decided that I needed to do something different. I can't honestly tell you that religion made me change because I was pretty angry. I felt, "God why did you do this to me? Why have you thrown this at me to change what might have been the life I had perceived for myself, not really knowing exactly what that was. Why have you put all these obstacles in front of me? Life is no fun." But I decided that I had too long ahead of me to cry about that. And so I decided I was going to have a change of scenery because Denver wasn't working for me, although I had a lot of friends there.

So I decided I was going to San Diego. Originally, it was Hawaii, but they had a quarantine on the dog and I wasn't going to put my dog in a cage for six months. So I said alright San Diego. Beach, warm weather, no more snow like I grew up in, no more snow like in Denver, occasionally — maybe a fresh start. So I went out one night. It was a blizzard, and only idiots and drunks were out. I'm not sure which I was, but take your pick. But I met two guys who said let's go to another bar, so I thought okay, whatever. They were from Tennessee and they talked kind of funny, you know. So I went with them. And there were a couple of ladies there that I met, and I decided to go out with one of them, and she and I hit it off and I thought this is nice, but I'm leaving. And I still did leave, but this lady helped me move to San Diego, helped me find a place to live, stayed in touch, and about six months after I moved out here in mid-1976, Janice came out. And she's still with me. And well, that was nice and I'm thanking God for that.

So when I came to San Diego, I got still more involved and determined to make a change in the way I was living my life. I eventually got a job with the Veterans Administration working with veterans. I decided I didn't want to do that anymore. I wanted to take the Bar exam and be a lawyer here. I did go to law school. So I took the Bar, but I'd also been getting involved with the Blinded Veterans Association, a national organization of blinded veterans and I eventually rose to be its national President, which is where I met Admiral Edney at the Salute to Veterans when Bush 41 was inaugurated. But I got involved — I got to know people — I was offered an opportunity to open a Vietnam

Veterans Leadership Program Office here in San Diego, so I did that for about a year-and-a-half, but I decided that I did not want to be a professional veteran. I really wanted to try to do something with my law. I borrowed money from the SBA, $50,000.00 and blew that in a year. I didn't get enough clients and eventually paid that loan back. Ed Miller finally offered me an opportunity to be a prosecutor with the District Attorney's Office, so I joined that office in '86 and did that for 12 years and I had a lot of fun being a trial lawyer and doing everything that prosecutors do. And I thought I would like to at least try to finish my career as a judge, although finishing as a prosecutor would have been okay. I applied to the Governor's Office and it will be 15 years in March that Governor Wilson appointed me to the bench and I'm still there, and there is 946 days left until I retire. But who's counting? (Laughter)

So that's kinda where my career has gone and if I can be so bold as to be showing some stupid arrogance here — this perspective comes from understanding and hopefully wisdom — I look back over my life and I was thinking you know I was not very happy with what I thought God did to me, but I thought "Gee I've turned out okay. I've been successful. Maybe it's time for me to forgive God for what he did to me." And the more I thought about it, I said, "Who am I — a lowly little human being to forgive God?" In looking at the blessings I've had through my life, the love of my wife, my family, the support that I've received, the opportunities that have come to me, I should be asking God to forgive me for not keeping the faith with him.

Edward's asking me to do this has really forced me to give some thought to that. A lot of obstacles were put in my path and maybe for a reason. I'm beginning to think that God knew that he was going to be there to help me over these hurdles, the stumbles that I've had, and I'm going to go through the rest of my life thinking that there was a purpose for all of this and my faith is stronger for that. I'm reminded of a verse I read from 2nd Timothy, Chapter 4, Verse 7, I think it is, where he said, "I have fought the good fight." And I guess I'm still, in some ways, fighting a little bit of a fight, but the big battles for me are over. I don't even think there are any skirmishes anymore. I know a lot of you say "Well if you found God again, how come you don't come to church every Sunday?"